Thank You Yesterday and So Long Tomorrow

A Guide for Living in the Now

Elizabeth Crooks

Thank You Yesterday and So Long Tomorrow: A Guide for Living in the Now

Copyright © 2016 Elizabeth Crooks

ISBN: 069236823X

ISBN-13: 978-0692368237

Cover by Elizabeth Crooks

For more information please visit:

www.elizabeth-crooks.com

DEDICATION

To all my family, friends and every other soul I've had the honor of crossing paths with on this journey. We are all teachers and we are all students, so thank you for sharing in this experience we call life.

I also dedicate this book to Fear; for without you, this book would never have been published.

CONTENTS

"There is a time for being ahead, a time for being behind; a time for being in motion, a time for being at rest; a time for being vigorous, a time for being exhausted; a time for being safe, a time for being in danger. The Master sees things as they are, without trying to control them. She lets them go on their own way, and resides at the center of the circle."

Lao Tzu, Tao de Ching

AUTHOR INTRODUCTION

I was sitting on a bench outside watching the sunrise one summer day, covered in mosquito bites from the hike I took the day before, when I came up with the idea for this book. My calves were blanketed in red bumps, throbbing from the itch as well as my failed attempts to not scratch them. That's what I get for hiking barefoot and in shorts through a forest I thought. I was entirely exhausted that morning, having cried all night.

I was on a retreat to work through my emotions. Ha! Not only were we trying to work on releasing our emotions but to show gratitude in every moment. I was having a hard time being grateful for becoming an all-you-can-eat mosquito buffet the day before but I decided to give it a try. Through all the discomfort I managed to say "thank you, yesterday." But that got me thinking...yesterday, literally, was just the day before. Why shouldn't I be grateful for every yesterday I've ever experienced? And that is where this book comes in.

My intent with writing this book is to share my personal experiences with learning to let go of the past, appreciating the past, overcoming fears of the future, and living in the now. I don't claim to know all the answers. I just know what has helped me over the years of my own spiritual enlightenment and personal discovery.

As humans we all learn from each other. We observe and try

new things. Sometimes they don't work out and other times we are pleasantly surprised at the suggestions and successes of others we've encountered along our life path.

It took me a long time to figure out what "living in the now" meant. I tried meditation to quiet the thoughts in my head: the worries of the future and the thoughts of the past; regret, anger, shame, betrayal, guilt; of the people and things that didn't matter anymore. What does it mean to live in the now anyway? Is it really that easy to just let go of the past? Part of the human struggle pertains to holding onto the past: the heartaches, the joy, and the choices we've made that have made us who we are today.

My job is to get you to think, as others have done for me. It helps to have multiple perspectives on how to live in the now. I can tell you what to do, and it might work for a little while, but until you can come to these conclusions on your own you won't fully comprehend and incorporate change into your daily life.

There are no right or wrong answers anymore. There is no single path to happiness. We are on a unique journey. No two paths are the same. And we're all walking multiple paths at one time. The goal is to expand your mind, expand your possibilities, and incorporate changes into your lives through observation and knowledge.

Use this guide as another tool in your own personal and spiritual development. Take what resonates with you and apply it to your own life. There may be things that don't resonate with you and that's okay too. I share in the belief that at least one person will benefit from this information. If you think something in this book will help another, a friend or family member, please pass it on.

And don't accept this as the end all, be all. Don't take anything as the ultimate truth. We each have to find our own truth, come to our own conclusions. These words I write helped me on my own path and I wish to share them with you. Please do not substitute the information within this book for professional advice, medical or otherwise.

We are meant to be free. We are meant to be happy. So enjoy this present moment.

LIVING IN THE NOW

What does it mean to live in the now? Conscious thought.

Consciously thinking is being aware of your thoughts, paying attention to them, and having the mindfulness to change them, if needed, in every moment. It is focusing on what you want and not of the wants of others. Living in the now means that everything is done with intention. Living in the now means letting go of the past and not worrying about the future. We get to choose what life we want to live right now.

Be aware of the life you are living and if it is your own. This may seem like a silly awareness at first. Well of course I'm living my own life! Whose other life could I be living? You'd be surprised at the answer. Are you doing what you truly want to do? Are you happy? Happiness is a major indicator on whose life you are living. Start thinking about where you are unhappy. Are you stuck in the past or are you stuck in a future that will never happen?

In order to become conscious we need to become aware first. One can't change without knowing they can change in the first place.

This book will help you sort through your thoughts, your dreams, and guide you into releasing the ones that no longer serve your best interest. We tend to suppress our true passions because we've been told they will never make any money or because we worry about what others will think of us if we do this or that. Sort through your fears and your belief systems to find the real you. We are all unique and we each have our own gift. Happiness is not only discovering that gift but using it each and every moment.

You are solely responsible for your own happiness. Living in the now means you consider yourself to be just as important. There is a sense of courage in letting go of the past, for it isn't an easy thing to do. Overcoming your fears won't be a picnic either. If you want change you have to start now.

We'll expand on this later.

THE HUMAN MIND

The human mind is a powerful thing. It can believe anything it wants to. It can be conditioned to think one way over another. We change our minds all the time, whether we follow new trends or forge our own. We learn what we like and what we don't like through repetition. We base our actions on what we think and what we believe. Beliefs are just collections of thoughts. And the mind controls our thoughts.

The mind also has the power to keep us prisoner to a thought or to set us free. If you believe in limits you are limited. How do you see yourself? Do you see unlimited potential? Do you see perfection?

All possibilities lie right outside your belief system. Pick apart your mind, your thoughts, and see how messed up they truly are. The more you can see, the more you can change. I'm not saying this is an easy thing to do. A lot of things are easier said than done. But it is possible. From here on out we're going to question our thoughts so we can let go of the past and the future.

There is only so much the mind can do though. I could describe what an apple tastes like, but you would have no idea what that really means until you experience an apple for yourself. The mind will take what it knows and paint a picture, an assumption, on what an apple is and how it tastes, until it "knows" for sure.

Even if you tried one apple, there are several other varieties that taste different. And if your first experience with an apple is traumatic, whether it was rotten or it hit you in the head, you may not want to give another apple a fair try.

It's All in Your Mind

Psychosomatic, or "it's all in the mind," is a term we use to describe the psychological phenomenon of creating reality with just a thought.

Have you ever made yourself sick on purpose? I used to do it all the time to get out of work. I was under the impression when I first started working that one actually had to be sick in order to call out sick from work. So when I really didn't want to go, I would end up getting really sick. I didn't put two and two together at the time.

Later I learned, through observing my co-workers and generally not liking being sick, one could call out sick without *actually* being sick. Come on, you know you've done it, or thought about doing it. And if you haven't, well, good for you then. I'm admitting it. Thoughts and beliefs are powerful things.

This kind of thinking happens all the time, both subconsciously and unconsciously. Has your mom ever told you that you'd catch a cold if you didn't wear a hat outside? And whenever it's cold outside do you not think about the fact you are not wearing a hat like you should be and have a fleeting thought of possibly getting sick from it? I didn't get the hat story as much as the one about going out in the cold with wet hair would make me sick.

Would you believe any of this if no one ever told you to? We have programs running we aren't even aware of. A comment from some random person we met once as a child could have created an entire series of thoughts and beliefs that shaped how we think today. It's all in there, and it can also be reversed. Knowing how your mind works will let you override the programs that keep you trapped to a thought or a set of thoughts that are preventing you from living in the now to the fullest.

The Ego

There is a difference between the mind and the ego. There are many ways to define the ego, and it is really hard to do so properly, but here is one explanation:

The ego is the false you. It is the identities we've created. It is our logical side: calculating, evaluating. It is our survival mechanism. The ego keeps us safe by controlling the thoughts and information we come to believe. Survival is its number one priority and it will achieve that by any means necessary, especially lying to you. It does such a good job keeping us alive that it prevents us from experiencing life to the fullest.

Your mind, on the other hand, is what you might call free will. The mind is the other part of you, the part that dreams and decides what to do next. The mind likes to imagine all the possibilities. The ego lets you know if that dream or decision is "realistic."

The ego is also in charge of duality: the good and the bad; the light and the dark; right and wrong. It is the little voice at the back of your mind that questions everything. It's the voice that says you can't do something. The ego worries about money, about time. The ego is what keeps you up at night. The ego ruins a moment.

The mind could care less because everything is simply an experience. The mind is neutral. The ego places values on experiences, has them weighed and measured against the highest of standards. It keeps you from trying things over. And it never lets you forget. But you can forgive. *You* can move on. Because you are not your ego.

The ego is only a part of the mind. It ultimately teaches us that we are not our thoughts, our beliefs. We are not what we wear or how we style our hair. We are not the job we do or the hobbies we pursue. Do not believe everything your mind thinks. We are perfect just as we are. We know we are more than our minds, our bodies. You are not your mind because you are aware of your mind as a separate entity. The ego keeps us separated from our true selves, and that is why we often feel lost or depressed. The ego isn't a bad guy. It just has a job to do. And it does a damn good job at it.

The ego wants an explanation to everything. The mind wants to jump at opportunities, try new things. Trust is something that isn't easily accepted nowadays. But in order to grow we need to learn to trust again.

Open your heart, clear out old thoughts, and expand your mind. You will expand your possibilities. We feel powerless to the thoughts of our egos, but now it is time to break down those thoughts and see just how ridiculous they really are.

THOUGHTS

Thoughts are the basis of our belief systems. Our lives are made up of all the thoughts we've had over our lifetimes, as well as the thoughts of others. Sometimes we believe in things instantly (no time required), while other beliefs are formed over longer periods of time.

One could argue that thoughts are the basic units of existence. After all, thoughts are just energy. You spend the same amount of energy making yourself miserable as you do making yourself happy. We can even feel trapped by our own thoughts; feel like prisoners to our own minds. If you're thinking you're getting the same old reality day in and day out, then that is what you perceive day in and day out: the same old stuff.

If you believe in limits, then you are limited. You have unlimited potential; untapped and unrealized. All you have to do is change your thoughts and you'll change your world.

This takes a constant commitment, for many thoughts and beliefs have been built over time, have many emotional attachments to them, so they take more effort to change. But it can be done. In order to embrace living in the now, many years of old thoughts need to be let go of or altered. All things are possible if you believe they are.

Belief Systems

They say the sky is the limit. The real limit is your belief system. Thoughts repeat to form our beliefs. Usually our beliefs have been inherited through other people: things we've heard, things we've been told to believe, and things we've been told not to believe. And we tend to believe things easier when they get told repeatedly. If everyone thinks it, it must be right...right?

Here is a good tip: Don't believe everything you think.

Remember the ego? It has its own line of thinking. Its belief system is: survival at all costs. It keeps us in fear mode so we don't do anything to interfere with our survival, both physical and mental. Everyone has their own ego looking out for them. We all believe differently. But we tend to share similar beliefs with other people. But then we can also have very different beliefs about certain things.

Just like our thoughts, beliefs don't necessarily define who we are. Thoughts and beliefs change all the time. *We* change all the time. It is our reaction to our own thoughts and the thoughts of others that truly define who we are.

Our ability to change our thoughts in any moment is what makes us human. Thoughts dictate the experiences we have in our lifetimes. Beliefs can keep us stuck in a moment and beliefs can let us live life to the fullest.

What did you think of vegetables growing up? I hated vegetables as a child. From what I see in the media, most other children hate vegetables too. My Mom was always telling me to eat my vegetables. Cartoons told me to eat my vegetables. I was a bread and potato girl. Salt and pepper were my main spices growing up.

I had to wait until my mid-twenties before I was able to try red bell peppers over and over again until I actually liked them. After learning how to cook a wider array of vegetables and expanding my spice palate, what I eat now has changed dramatically. But why do people hate things they have never tried? I still refuse to try certain foods because of what I think they might taste like. It's kind of silly if you really think about it.

How about this: have you ever been told you're too young to do something? How about too old? Well, who says? Often we believe we're too young, too old, too tall, too fat, too this and too that to do something. We never seem to be "just right." We call this the goldilocks syndrome. We find it hard to believe we're perfect in every moment. But this is just a belief system.

Actually everything is perfect, if you believe it is. We tend to judge the experience without realizing that every experience is perfect just as it is. The next time you believe you can't do something, question why. Is it a thought someone else has told you? Or is it your own mind doubting itself?

Automated Programs

Think of the mind as a computer. Most of our thoughts are just automatic programs running in the background. It's like we're running on autopilot most of the time. We wake up, we get dressed, we get ready for the day (or night), we do this and we do that. The stuff we've done all our lives are still thoughts, still beliefs, running around in our heads. We've just tuned them out.

Here is a simple scenario to get you thinking:
You're at a dinner party with family. You grab Mom's favorite sweet potato dish served in Grandma's antique bowl to bring it to the table when you accidentally trip, drop the dish, splatter sweet potato across the room and shatter Grandma's dish.

Now, what was your first thought? Were you embarrassed? Were you angry at yourself? Did you try to blame it on someone else? Did you think you were a horrible person? That you were stupid?

In situations like this, and in all of our daily experiences, the trick is to recognize the thoughts and emotions that come up and pick them apart. Don't try and stop the thought or the emotion. That is impossible. See the automatic programs as they are so you can work on changing them. Next time those thoughts come up, consciously change them.

As for the dinner party, accidents happen. No one is to blame. There is no one to get angry at. You are a perfect being. Whatever happened was an experience, a lesson, nothing more. Perhaps it was time to buy new dishes anyway.

We've attached thoughts/emotions to many things. Anger, betrayal, guilt, shame, embarrassment, etc. can come up at the strangest of times. If you're thinking: "why the hell did that (thought) come up?" then you are on the right track. Work on seeing what comes up and when. Once you realize where a thought is coming from, why you got embarrassed or why you got angry, you can let go of that thought and change it to one where you did nothing wrong.

We'll work on this throughout the rest of the book.

Words

Words are the basic unit of thought. Start paying attention to the words you tell yourself. What comes up when you *drop* something? How do you feel when you *fail* a test? When you *overcook* something? When your drive-thru order is *wrong*? How you react to a word determines what that word means to you.

Words have power. Words *are* power. Listen to what words you use in every moment. Listen to what you tell yourself and what words you use with other people. What comes to mind when you look in a mirror? Why do you say the things that you do? That is mindfulness.

I invite you to research the work of Dr. Masaru Emoto and his findings on the effects of words, music and other expressions on water crystals on your own if you find it interesting. The power of simple words and intention is truly amazing. If you want to experience this for yourself, I offer an experiment to try at home.

The Three Little Words Experiment

A fun little experiment to try is to write the words *"I Love You"* and *"I Hate You"* on two separate pieces of paper and tape them to the glass jars of two identical flowers or bouquets of flowers.

Use glass or any clear jar/vase instead of translucent plastic. And make sure the words are facing the inside of the container, so that you can read the words through the water. Be sure to treat both flowers the same: put them in the same amount of sunlight and have the same water level. Leave them alone for a while and see if the two flowers change over time.

Another variation is to cook a batch of white rice and separate it out into two clear glass jars (with a lid). Tape "*I Love You*" to one jar, with the words facing the rice, and tape "*I Hate You*" to the other jar. Make sure the rice is sealed and leave it in a cool, dark spot. See if you can spot any changes over time.

Now, at the end of the experiment your mind may not believe what it sees. No matter how well you set it up, you might think you did something wrong. Maybe the flowers got too cold or got too much sun. Maybe the rice wasn't sealed properly. And then, perhaps, you'll believe in the power of three little words.

TIME

At its core, time is an illusion. Time is relative, subjective, and is different for everyone at every moment. Time speeds up and slows down; it seems to fly by and then stop completely. Two people can experience time side-by-side and it'll appear differently for each person.

One moment can appear to last forever and the next moment can be gone before you know it. Time can be expressed in numbers on a clock, as being too late or too early, as day and night, and as yesterdays and tomorrows. At one point in time there were thirteen months in a year. Time is not fixed.

"Yesterday" and "tomorrow" are perceptions of the mind, and we use time to justify them as going in one direction or the other. The concept of "now" is another matter. We are all living in a single moment, or an infinite number of moments, and it is the human mind that perceives that moment as expanded over "time."

By the time you have finished reading this section several moments will have past. "Now" could be described as living in a moment that isn't concerned with either a past or a future. All that matters is now, and now is all that matters.

The Waiting Game

There is a debate on whether time makes things worse or

better. Well, it all depends on how you look at it. Time will work for you in the way you believe it to. Time can heal, or time can destroy. And it can do both at the same time. There is the old adage that says time heals all wounds. Since time is subjective to our own experiences, wounds can appear to heal faster or slower than another, while others appear to heal instantaneously.

In regards to mental and emotional wounds, we can't rely on time to heal them for us. We have to make the choice to do so, here and now. Not "tomorrow." We're good at playing the waiting game. We wait for others to come around, to call, to apologize, to show us appreciation, to show us love. Why do we wait? Why not take matters into our own hands and appreciate ourselves for who we are, now.

If now is all there is, we can love ourselves for who we are in this moment. We can be happy in this moment. We don't have to wait for the time to change or for the time to be right. We just have to find that power within and start using it.

Limited Time

Time is really just a limit. We put ourselves into little time boxes. We have deadlines and parameters for success and failure. We judge ourselves and others through time: the young verses the old. We think things like: "If I'm not married by age 25, no one will ever love me," and "If I don't own a house with a white picket fence right out of college then I'm not really successful." How crazy are these lines of thought? You are not too young or too old to do something. You are not a failure at anything. Time is irrelevant.

How much time do you want to spend regretting the past (that which you cannot change), and how much time do you want to spend thinking about the future (and worrying about the one that will never happen)?

We tend to spend a lot of our time in any moment other than this one. We re-play all the regret, the anger, the sadness, the loss, the "what ifs," the good days, and the bad days. Is that how you want to live the rest of your life? If so that is okay. Some people are not ready to let go of the past. And some people like waiting for a future that is not meant to be.

Think of yesterday as daytime and tomorrow as nighttime. Every moment is now, whether it is light with the sun out and blue skies, or dark with the stars and moonlight. The human mind separates out day and night, yesterday and tomorrow, in order to make sense of time, to make sense of life. The illusion of this separation keeps one limited to all the possibilities that lie in the now.

We've experienced many yesterdays, and we'll experience many tomorrows. What we choose to do in the now will always be time well spent.

Although time is an illusion, we have to play with it in order to function in day-to-day life. The point is not to get too concerned over time, to not to let it consume you. Use the concept of time to your advantage when focusing on being in the now to the fullest.

LIFE AS A STORY

Life has all the aspects of a story: a list of characters, an overall theme, plot twists and turns, foreshadowing futures, flashbacks to the past, separate chapters, and new editions written over time. We write and re-write our stories in every moment. The trick is to become a conscious writer and take control of your personal story instead of letting outside influences and your own subconscious mind write it for you.

There are many theories to life; what it means and what our purpose is here on Earth. Perhaps the purpose to life is to experience as many things as possible. And we experience life as a long story, or a memoir of sorts. Some parts of the story are already written for us and the rest we write as we go along.

Changing the words, the thoughts, changes the story. And we each have the power to do so. What story releases you from the past? What story frees you from a future you do not want? What story are you living in this moment?

We tend to be so concerned about other people's stories. It's an escape from our own. We focus on how much other people have and what they don't have, what they do and don't do, so we can feel better about our own lives.

When we judge another's story what we are really doing is judging our own. Life gives us experiences. All we can ask is, "what did I learn from it?" There is no need to judge what we experience. The world is a stage and all you are doing is playing a role.

Play with the possibility that your life is just a play, a story. Play with the thoughts in your head. Ask yourself why you have come to believe in certain things and not others. You can choose the story you live in every moment, you just have to believe you can.

Subjectivity

Everyone is living their own story. Everyone has their own definition of what it means to live, what it means to die, and everything in between. What makes one person angry makes another person laugh. What makes for a so-called "perfect" day is entirely different for two people. Even then, our stories change in every moment.

Details change in every moment. We identify with our stories, but a lot of the time we forget that the story changes. Identities change. All we are is the writer behind the story. We write the story, we change the story, we edit the story, and we live the story.

Only you can live your story.

And while we are living our own stories we should be mindful and respectful of other people's stories. As you are responsible for the choices you make in life, other people are responsible for the choices they make. We like to offer up our opinions, our judgments, our stories, to others in an attempt to impose on their life stories. Our perception of suffering comes from the expectation of others to see the world exactly as we do, to think the same way as we do. Our story is our own.

Have you heard of the expression there are two sides to every story? Actually it's more like there are two different stories to every side. Sometimes stories overlap. We share characters and plot lines. More than one person can have their stories intertwine for periods of time. And those same people can have their story lines unravel at later points along their life paths. Next time you're in a situation where there is more than one "side" to a story remember that we each have our own story with our own thoughts and experiences.

So, what story releases you from your past? What story frees you from the future you worry about? What story do you *want* to live in this current moment?

THANK YOU YESTERDAY

LETTING GO OF THE PAST

Letting go and losing something are two different things. We fear losing things. What we often miss seeing are the things we gain when we choose to let go. Letting go of the past isn't about cutting ties or forgetting memories or giving up a piece of ourselves. It's about getting okay with what has happened in your life. It's about releasing the emotional attachments that keep you stuck and prevent future growth.

Emotional pain is often worse than physical pain. All of the emotional experiences we've had in our lives make us who we are today. Our identities are held in the past. And it is often difficult to detach one's true self from the identities we created over time, through the countless experiences. Why are you the person you are in this moment? What has happened in your life to get you where you are today? If you take the 'positive' and 'negative' out of the equation, everything that happens in life is just an experience, a neutral event that our human ego decided to put a label on.

In the moment it's hard to see the experience for what it is, but later you'll look back on it and understand why you experienced it the way you did.

Our peace of mind is the ultimate goal. Having happiness in every moment should be the only expectation. And you can let go of all the thoughts that say otherwise. If you can let go of it then you don't really need it. Can you let go of happiness, love, and inner peace? Change your thoughts and you change your world. And since your thoughts are more than likely still linked to the past, it is the past we must work with first in order to live happily in the now.

So, how do you let go?

You get fed up and decide to do so. Consciously choose to make a big change, perhaps *the* biggest change in your life. And that is to let go of the old: the old beliefs, the old programs that have trapped you in a life you wish would change. Only one person has the power to change your life, and that is you.

Make peace with your past:

What are the words you have always wanted to hear, the words that you have never been told? The words, "I love you," are often not heard enough in our lives, especially from ourselves. Why are you angry with someone? Is it because they never said something you wanted to hear? Tell yourself what you need to hear in this moment. Look in a mirror and say: 'I love you,' 'You're beautiful,' 'You are perfect.'

Forgive yourself:

Accept all the parts of yourself. Accept all the events that made you who you are today. Suffering is a choice. Forgive yourself if needed. Apologize to another if needed. Saying 'I'm sorry' is just as powerful as saying 'I love you.'

Cry:

Yes, I said cry. Even men should cry. Whoever said that boys don't cry was just repeating someone else's thought.

In order to release an emotion one must cry it out. Feel it. Thank it. Let it go. Crying gets it out of the body; all of the emotions, thoughts, fears, feelings, habits, beliefs, and limits are just energy that needs to be released. Thank your tears for carrying those thoughts out of the body.

Cry if you have to. If others tell you to stop crying it is because they are uncomfortable with it. It has nothing to do with you. If you feel like crying, cry. There is nothing to be ashamed about. We are taught shame. We shame others out of our own fears, our own discomfort. Get okay with crying if you are not already. Crying is a good thing. The whole point is to feel the emotion, the energy, and get it out of the body so it doesn't continue to affect every moment of your life.

Start Small:

Start small with letting go. The big stuff will be harder to let go of at first. And by the big stuff I mean the stuff that has been with you since childhood: all the thoughts and belief systems of generations built up over time.

Letting go, or releasing the thoughts and emotions, can literally suck and feel like hell when you're going through it. Trust and believe it will all pass. The more miserable you feel the more freeing it will be afterwards.

Think of the expression: there is no use crying over spilled milk. It's just milk...

Pay Attention:

Memories reinforce feelings. Pay attention to what memories, thoughts, and beliefs come up. Don't' get stuck in the memory. There are always multiple angles. You may remember being angry in the past, but look around and see what else you might have felt. See your thoughts in many ways.

Break it all down. Notice themes and core beliefs that keep resurfacing. Be mindful of your thoughts. Awareness is the start to living in the now.

Outdated Beliefs

Why are all the emotions in the past? Behaviors are learned over time. We're taught to feel a certain way. We fear the very thought of what loss, anger, shame, etc. *could* feel like if we were ever to experience it. Maybe we saw someone cry as a child and we didn't want to feel that way ourselves. No one wants to feel pain. We avoid it. But we've felt what we couldn't avoid and put labels on those feelings.

Suffering is just a perception. Sometimes we have to "suffer" through the discomfort to learn comfort, live through the anger to learn peace. The only person responsible for our own suffering is our own self. Just look at the range of emotions one can feel, and the degrees to which can be felt. The human mind thinks it's experiencing a multitude of emotions when it's just putting conditions on which emotion is felt in each moment.

Pay attention to your emotions. What makes you sad? What makes you angry? Guilty? Happy? Lonely? And why? Only you can answer these questions.

Piece together the puzzle that is your own mind, how it works, why it thinks the way it does, which experiences have defined your life and your emotions. Then choose if you want to believe that anymore. It is your choice to continue to experience anger, sadness, regret, shame, etc. in every moment, or to experience something new.

However, you can't change the past. What's done is done. But you can change your thoughts about it. You can choose how you will react from this point in time and onward. You have to decide whether to let the past define your thoughts, or to change the thoughts about your past.

APPRECIATING THE PAST

This is one of the hardest things you'll do when letting go of the past. We all have things we regret, things that made us sad or angry or happy. Showing gratitude for everything that has happened in your life up to this point, all of the good memories and all the perceived sufferings, can be hard to do. Why should we be grateful for all the times we perceive as 'bad'?

It helps to remember that everything is just an experience. Thank the past for showing you anger, betrayal, guilt, sadness, addiction, loss, happiness, love. Thank the past for teaching you how to express those emotions, those thoughts. Appreciate the past for what it is. Appreciate all the people who pushed your buttons, who showed you the 'dark' side of yourself and those who showed you the light, who taught you patience and those that tested it. Even if you want change, thank the past for what it's done to shape you into the person you are in this moment.

One cannot let go of the past without appreciating it. Resenting the past only gives it permission to continue having control over your life. Being grateful for everything life has given you, and will continue to give you in every moment, is essential for living in bliss and living in the now. The point is to let go of everything that no longer serves your best interest. It may be very hard to appreciate things at first, but hopefully this book will help get you on the path to letting go of the past and attachments to the future that are causing discomfort in life.

Thank Everything

One of the things that helped me get into the mindset of being grateful for everything in my life was to start thanking everything I saw. Thank the sun for shining. Thank the trees (they provide oxygen, energy, nutrition, paper products). Thank the stars at night. Say thank you to your body, it's the vessel that allows you to experience this journey. Spend time with it, listen to it, and nourish it with yummy foods. Say thank you in more ways than one. By the laws of the universe, when you give thanks you get thanks in return.

Thankfulness is not just a casual thought; it should be expressed in every moment. Consciously thank all the thoughts that come to mind. You can choose to start changing those thoughts, but also thank them for being there. They are giving you the opportunity to look at them and choose whether to believe them or not from here on out. You have fear, anger, sadness, etc... Accept it. Those emotions, those thoughts, exist. Don't fight them. Say "thank you for being there but you are no longer needed."

ATTACHMENT

"The root of suffering is attachment"
-Buddha

I've heard this saying several times over my lifetime. I never really understood it before either. I took it literally and gave away a lot of my 'stuff' for free and cleaned up a lot of mindless clutter from my life. Maybe it improved my happiness and mental state for a while…but then, what is left after all the stuff is gone?

Your mind is still there. Your thoughts are still there. Why did I give away all my stuff? Why can't I buy more stuff? That guy over there with all my old stuff is happy now…why am I not happy?

I do believe that attachment is one of the reasons for human suffering. We tend to cling to things beyond their usefulness. The human mind attaches memories to objects. This is why people tend to buy so many souvenirs on their many travels.

But those happy memories can keep us stuck thinking of a time long past. Things our exes gave us. Things our grandparents gave us. We think that if we give something away, or never purchase a memento in the first place, that the person, place or thing never really existed. We have to prove we visited some place. We have to prove we loved some person. We have to have proof that we were loved by someone else. That is the kind of attachment that leads to suffering.

So, how attached are you to your stuff? If you had to pick up and go with all the belongings you couldn't bear to part with, how easy would that be?

One of the ways I had to let go of the past was to purge most of my belongings. I started with yard sales, rarely selling anything because I asked too much for my things. I was holding on. Then, begrudgingly at first, I began to take small piles of stuff to donate. Sometimes I would give myself a hard time about it afterwards. Other times I went out and re-bought items I previously parted with. Over time I found I was releasing more and more stuff and caring less and less about it. What I did have left was useful. But I still kept a few things that reminded me of a few past moments: a stuffed animal my Dad bought me, a few pictures from my childhood, and some jewelry I made with friends.

It's hard to part with things. We attach memories to objects, emotions both good and bad. See where you are struggling to let go. See what is really important to you by looking at what you own. Some things may represent moments that we want to let go of. And it'll be up to you to decide if letting go of that item will help let go in your mind.

Expectations

Not only do we become attached to physical objects, but we attach our own perceptions and ideals on other people. We project our expectations onto others. And we're often disappointed when those people are not who we want them to be.

Things change. People change. But rarely do we realize that everyone reveals their true selves to others over time. It's a safety mechanism. We reveal pieces of ourselves slowly so not to scare other people away. We want to impress others so we say things we don't mean, do things we don't actually like doing, in order to create an image. When the illusion of that image is shattered we feel betrayed, angry, sad…all ranges of emotion.

After all, the people closest in our lives are just an extension of our selves. Actually all people in the world are extension of ourselves. We expect others to act as we do, to believe as we do. We expect the world to work a certain way and we get emotional when it doesn't work out that way.

Emotions, or thoughts, are created when our expected reality is different than actual reality. Expectations attach emotions to outcomes. If I don't get this I'll be angry, sad, or happy. If this happens, or if that happens, then I'll feel this way or that way. Your expectations and attachments need to be let go of as well in order to truly live in the moment.

The point is to get okay with anything happening at any moment. So you expected someone to apologize and they didn't. You expected that guy to not cut you off in traffic. You expected to have your favorite muffin waiting for you at the local bakery and it wasn't. If you're only going to be happy if all the pieces of your life fit into a neat little box of your own limited design, well then you are never going to be happy.

Our expectations and what actually happens are rarely equal. Ride the ride, play along in the play. Happiness is letting go of the expectations and enjoying what is, for what it is.

ANGER

Anger, in all its forms, is created from within. From annoyance and frustration, to bitterness and resentment, to being totally blinded by anger, anger comes up often in life.

All of these emotions are crafted internally from perceived wrongdoings and suffering: expectations and attachments to outcomes. We get angry when something doesn't go 'our' way. We get angry when things aren't going 'right.' Have you ever been or seen someone so angry you just want to laugh? It certainly isn't funny in the moment. But that is why anger is easy to let go of.

Are you an angry person? Know someone who tends to be angry all the time? There is only person who can "help" an angry person, and that is themselves. If you've ever tried to talk to an angry person, you'd know the last thing they want to hear is something along the lines of "calm down". Why? Because we don't think we should have to calm down.

We project our anger onto other people and other things. People have to look within to figure out why they are so angry, which is something that is hard for most of us to do. But if you want to get over the anger, to truly let it go, you have to look within yourself.

So here is one way to look at it: Anger is never at another, it is at ourselves.

I'll say it again: *Anger is never at another, it is at ourselves.* All anger is directed at our own selves, although we project and perceive it to be towards another person or thing. Somewhere we are either self-judging or compromising in some way.

And little compromises add up. For example, you really want a hamburger and your boyfriend/girlfriend is a vegetarian and so you start eating cheese pizza all the time. It doesn't seem like a big deal at first. But after five years of being 'denied' a hamburger you may start to resent some things. Now this is an extreme and ridiculous example, but listing all the ways we compromise ourselves everyday would be even more ridiculous.

Compromising over time leads to anger…anger at ourselves for not speaking our truth or standing up for ourselves. We get angry when we're not doing what we want to do or when we feel like we can't do it for some reason. And we get angry when other people don't think like us or believe as we do. Other people's beliefs challenge the way we believe, and so doubt surfaces and we question ourselves, thinking *we're* wrong in some way, so we get angry and lash out at other people, believing they must be wrong because there is no way we can be wrong…and the cycle goes on and on.

Letting go of Anger

So, anger comes up. What do you do? Recognize the anger and choose to change it, or not. Look beyond the emotion to the thought, or thoughts, behind it. Work with your belief systems.

Most of the time, you'll find your thoughts to be so ridiculous that you'll wonder why you ever believed them in the first place.

We like to play the blame game with anger. It's not my fault I'm angry, it's because that guy cut me off in traffic, because my wife forgot our anniversary, because I got whole milk in my coffee instead of skim milk, because my favorite television show got canceled…

Blaming others for your life just means you've given your power away. You can take that power back by changing what you do and do not allow in your reality anymore. And it's also about both gaining control and letting go of control over your life at the same time. We can't control everything that goes on in our lives, but we do have control over how we react and respond to life. Be responsible for your own actions; your own thoughts; your own reality.

Just like all other emotions, you can't prevent future anger. You just have to go with the flow of it. Don't beat yourself up about it afterwards too. People get angry, accept it. It's what you do about it during and afterwards that matters most. So you got angry. Can you forgive yourself for it? Can you laugh it off? Can you think of ways not to have anger come up in future moment, or how to react better to it in the next one?

Start thanking the emotions that surface if you can. They'll be easier to release. Don't struggle or fight the emotion either. Surrender in a way. Take the power of the emotion away by not letting it control your life and your thoughts in this moment. You got angry, so what?

BETRAYAL

So, someone lied to you. Someone did something they said they weren't going to do. Someone said something personal about you to someone else. Your partner cheated on you. Your confidence, your trust, has been betrayed. So how do you feel? People go against their word all the time. That is their problem, not yours. Deception isn't "fun," but it happens, and you can choose to let it affect you or not.

One of the hardest things to do is to not take things personal. It's not about you. You can't expect others to think or do the same as you. Everyone has their own experiences, their own rule book they live by.

So someone hurt you by lying to you. It is not your fault what they did. Your only responsibility is how you respond and how you react. You don't have to play the victim. You don't have to feel bad about it. Although we value honesty and truth, we should remember things change. People change their minds. People's needs change. We each have our own definition of loyalty, and we feel betrayed when others' definitions don't match up.

Here is another thing to think about: It is not what they do, it is what I allow. You can allow others' actions and beliefs to interfere with your own. We allow things all the time subconsciously and unconsciously. We give permissions we are not aware of. You loan a movie out to a friend and never get it back. Well you were aware that that could happen on some level, whether you acknowledged it or not. If it really meant so much to you that you could never part with it, then you would never have loaned it out in the first place. We place our trust in believing other people think and act the same way as we do. And when they don't we feel betrayed. *They* weren't honorable; *they* weren't sincere; *they* betrayed *me*. Well, sorry, but you allowed them to do so. And you are allowing their actions, that event, to continue to affect your life. You can't control what others do. But you can control how you react when things happen.

Emotional Scars

Why do some wounds scar and others don't? Scars are merely reminders. When we let go of the importance that event holds within us, scars can literally dissolve away. No medical-emotional cream needed. I've worked with cats professionally and I've had cats apart of my family all my life. I've been scratched more times than I can remember and yet I only have one scar, and that is from my first cat scratch ever. At least it was the first one I remember someone telling me it was going to scar, and it did. Twenty years later I still have it.

Just like physical scars, we've set up reminders throughout our lives to show us our old emotions, old thoughts, and old programs. Songs remind us of the past. Places remind us of the past. We eat a certain food that reminds us of something we need to let go of. We could be stuck in a betrayal loop, seeing it everywhere, and in everything others do around us. We think things are being done *to* us, when it really is just our perception and fear of being out of control. Again, we can't control other people, but we can control our reactions. We can choose to let their actions scar us for life, or to let it go.

GUILT

Guilt is essentially the feeling we have when we're not living up to our own expectations or the perceived expectations of others and society. We also tend to feel guilty when we think we did something wrong. And we often feel guilty living life the way we want to.

Write this down and hang it up somewhere you look every day to remind you: "Don't let anyone make you feel guilty for living life your way."

Now, about the things you have done in the past, why does it make you feel guilty? Did you do something you weren't supposed to? Did you not do something you were supposed to? Thinking back on it now, remember that it is only a past moment. Whatever it was, it happened. That moment is gone. The moment happened exactly as it needed to. The ego likes to use guilt to keep us trapped in the past, unable to appreciate our current moment out of fear of guilt.

Have you made others feel guilty? You can let that go too. Apologize if you feel the need to. If you feel guilty each and every day for not doing something, then go do it. Let go of the moments you can no longer control. Say: "thank you for teaching me something about myself, but that experience is no longer necessary from this moment on." The only person making you feel guilty is you. Think about it. Get okay with whatever happened. Forgive yourself.

All you can ask of yourself is to do your best in every moment. Other people will say you didn't do enough for them. That is their perception. That is their issue. Don't give your power away by allowing other people to make you feel guilty. And also remember your own ego will try to do the same. Self-imposed guilt can be a little harder to let go of because the source of the guilt is within our own minds, our own thoughts. No one likes looking at themselves. No one wants to know why they think the way they do. But what's in the past is in the past.

Make your current moment free of guilt by working on your thoughts and how you view your actions and interactions with yourself and others.

SADNESS

Sadness: the opposite of happiness. If the only person that can make ourselves happy is ourselves, then sadness is just an emotion we allow ourselves to feel. We let things make us sad. We let our feelings get hurt by caring what other people think of us. It's all in the mind. Ultimately it is your choice to be sad. And it is your choice to be happy, or at least to attempt to find happiness in every situation. If you don't think you can find your way to happiness, beyond the sadness, then you have to work with that thought first. Ask yourself what it will take for you to be happy. Ask yourself if you truly want to be happy. Always remember you have a choice and the power to change your own thoughts.

So, how do you feel about your past? Nostalgia can have us looking at our past through rose-tinted glasses. We often cover up feelings of sadness with other emotions. I was indifferent a lot of my childhood. I bottled up all my emotions. I thought I was a pretty happy child, and most of the time I was. But the sad parts I covered up with anger, guilt, shame, regret.

The human mind filters out what it finds to be too uncomfortable to deal with. This "hurts" us more than we realize when we cover up the past. But not really. It just makes it a little more difficult to figure out what we need to let go of sometimes. If you can look kindly upon your past without judgment, then nostalgia is nothing more than a fond memory.

Work with all your memories, the ones you perceived as bad, as well as the good. Be thankful for how you felt at the time. Honor your feelings in this moment. If you feel like being sad, then be sad. But when you are tired of feeling that way, choose a new feeling in the new moment.

Loss

Sometimes sadness isn't even our own. Why do you feel sad? Are you sad for yourself or for another person or thing? Loss can make us feel sad for another. We've been conditioned to feel sadness at the loss of life. We even become emotional when we view loss through television or a movie. How do you feel when you experience loss? What do you think happens after the last chapter of your personal story is written?

We've all experienced loss in one way or the other. Losing a family member, friend or a pet is often more traumatic than seeing loss on the television or in the news. Either way your mind has processed loss in some way, whether it was to distance yourself from the pain or to throw yourself head first into that pain. And usually it's sadness that comes up at the thought of loss, although other emotions surface as well. Most of the time a myriad of emotions surface with every thought.

Whether you are dealing with loss in this moment, or can remember a moment from the past, see what emotions come up for you. You'll start to see the automatic programs, your core beliefs, when something as traumatic as loss happens in your life. So really think about what you feel when loss comes up and really work with those thoughts. We'll expand on loss later in the book.

ADDICTION

Those who are suffering due to loss, tragedy, rejection or abuse might distract themselves from that pain. The distraction can be so controlling over their life that they become addicted. We can't stand to be alone with our own thoughts, much less face our pains and fears.

I admit I'm a comfort eater. Food covered up my emotions for decades. I didn't think I could find comfort anywhere else. With all past traumas, whether physical, mental, or emotional, one needs to heal in order to let go. And by heal I mean to make whole again.

We're all addicted to something. It's just a matter of realizing it. Often we're addicted to things that don't make us feel good or happy. We may perceive it to be fulfilling at the time but those thoughts can be fleeting. Food makes one feel good until their body hurts. Continuous shopping for the next thing that will make one happy until they realize that all they have are things. Those who jump from relationship to relationship may not be satisfied with their life as it is and are often lonelier at the end of the day. Gambling can be seen as just hoping for a different outcome to life and relying on outside sources for happiness.

One has to find happiness within. One has to find peace within. Addiction is an endless search for something outside of oneself, an endless search for change that will never come because only we have the power to change our reality.

Thoughts

It is easier to recognize our physical addictions, but we often don't realize we become addicted to our thoughts. We also get addicted to talking about our perceived problems. There is a difference between talking about your problems and working through them. Talking while complaining and blaming others is not letting go.

Thought addictions manifest as physical addictions as well. Look at your actions and see the thoughts behind them. We can become addicted to things that make us feel like we're accomplishing something all the time, things that make us feel worthy. Playing video games all the time was an accomplishment for me. It made me feel like I made a difference in some world, although it wasn't my own. We all have ways of escaping from this life in one form or another.

One can get addicted to a certain kind of thinking. How often do others tell you you're not worthy? That you are stupid? That you don't matter? That you are anything but perfect? And how often do you tell yourself those things?

Emotional abuse, just like emotional pain, is often worse than the physical. The mind can be our prison, or it can set us free. *"Are you okay?"* is easily one of the dumbest questions ever. The real question is: *can* you get okay with it?

Can you get okay with whatever happened? Can you get okay with whatever will happen? Pain exists, but it is what you allow that pain to do to you that matters most. And you can let it go.

VICTIM MODE

There are two signs to being stuck in a victim mentality: complaining and whining. If you are complaining about something or whining about "poor little me" then you are playing the victim. People complain and whine when things happen out of their control. Either someone did something *to* you or you were wronged in some way. When you realize you've been stuck in victim mode, you can get yourself out of it by validating your feelings. Tell yourself you were right. Tell yourself they were wrong. What does it matter anyway?

Our egos like to tell us we're victims to circumstance, victims to events, and that we're even victims to our own thoughts. Validation is necessary sometimes in order to let go. If your ego is whining about something, you may need to be coddled and pitied. Instead of searching for pity elsewhere, give it to yourself. Or do you really want to be pitied in the first place? If you are claiming survivorship over something then you are acting the victim. If you are questioning, "why me?" then you are in victim mode. Validate yourself and move on.

Blame

Victims tend to blame the world for their problems. Victims like to think things are happening *to* them. You ever have one of those days where everything seems to go wrong? Like no matter what you do, everything you don't want to see happen keeps happening? You stub your toe getting out of bed. You put the wrong key in the lock and it gets stuck. Your grocery bag rips and your eggs break all over your loaf of bread. The air conditioning won't work on a hot day. You forgot your wallet at home. You get the idea.

We don't like to admit our part in life. We tend to point our fingers. We don't like to blame ourselves when things happen. But everything that happens in our lives is a result of our own thoughts. So we make everything happen in our lives whether we like it or not. It is easier to blame our problems on outside influences. But if everything seems to be going "wrong" in our lives, then that is our cue to stop and listen. Stop and think. Stop and take a breath. Take a moment to look really hard at your life. Why did all those things happen? Were you paying attention?

I fell down the stairs and sprained my toe at the beginning of last summer. It doesn't sound that bad but I couldn't walk without being in pain or limping for three weeks. The universe, my universe, wanted me to slow down and take a look at what I was doing. I was too focused on getting nowhere fast. I had no direction. As for falling down the stairs, it happened at night. I walked right past the light switch, even thought about turning it on. My intuition said to turn on the light but my ego said no, I could certainly walk down the stairs in the dark. Apparently I did need that light. I ignored my intuition and trusted my ego, my pride.

Listen to your intuition. Listen to your gut feelings. There is no one to blame, for anything. Not even your own mind. We choose our path in every moment. We just have to listen and take responsibility for what we do, without judgment.

OTHER EMOTIONS

I can't list every emotion or thought anyone has ever experienced that keeps them stuck in the past. But all emotions can be dealt with in similar ways. Remember attachments. If you have an emotion come up, you are attached. There is some energetic cord tying you to that person, place, or thing. All emotions are just attachments and expectations. See the emotion, see the thought behind it. Then work on cutting the energetic cords. Usually there are several cords attached to each emotion, each thought. You can cut one cord at a time or the entire marionette at once. It is your choice how you want to detach, to let go, if you want to at all.

Also remember that it can be very hard to cut the cords. We tend to not want to let go out of fear. We fear losing something; a piece of ourselves, memories of others and memories of places. Cutting the cord doesn't mean the memories go away (unless you want them to). The memories just become detached, like a picture in a frame on a wall you can look at from time to time, instead of dragging that picture around with you like a ball and chain.

Often the more traumatic the experience, the more thought energy needs to be worked with. Everyone has their own definition of what is traumatic and what isn't. More than one thought can be anchored to an experience.

Know that if you are talking to a friend or being the listener, remember that what may seem silly or ridiculous to you may be seriously traumatic for the other person. We all process things different and we all have different life events that influence the way we think and interpret the world.

Find the root cause of your emotion. It'll be different for everybody. There might be similarities between stories, but everyone has their own life experiences, memories and emotions attached to them. It is okay to say: "that's not me anymore." You have the power to change. As long as you understand why you are angry, sad, etc. then you can change it.

Embrace your emotions as well. Embrace them, love them, and then let them go. The only purpose emotions serve is to give you an experience. Thank them for the experience and move on to the next one.

If all there that exists is now, there would be no guilt, shame, regret…past moments would be just that, in the past. You can choose whether or not you want your emotions to affect you in the now. Whatever happened before doesn't matter now, and whatever you fear will happen in the future is not happening right now. We've played the game, created the story. Now is the time for a new game, a new story.

Jealousy

Several emotions, including jealousy, boil down to feeling worthless. When we're jealous, we're comparing ourselves to others. Our beliefs about attachments, our ideas of ownership, create feelings of jealousy. Are you envious of what another has? Why? With everything that exists in the world; all the choices and

57

options one could ever want, we tend to question our lives and look elsewhere for something 'better'. The grass isn't greener on the other side; it's just your perception that it is. If there is one question that could help with breaking down the feeling jealous of something or someone it would be this: *"Do you even know what you want?"*

Shame

We go to great lengths not to feel ashamed. We blend in with the crowd. We don't rock the boat. I never realized how much shaming I did to others on a subconscious level, and how much I was allowing others to do the same to me. People shame others to feel better about themselves. It often starts off as simple embarrassment, an opinion about another person's way of life. Maybe a joke about what they're wearing or what they're doing. Shame is simply self-judgment projected into public humiliation.

But people can only shame you if you let them. Embarrassment is a choice, although my auto-red cheek response might beg to differ. It took a very long time to realize I had nothing to be embarrassed about. Just like guilt, we allow others to question how we live our lives. So you tripped on the sidewalk. You had a piece of broccoli in your teeth when you gave that speech in class. You didn't realize your shirt was inside-out at work. So what? Who cares?

I'll share a memory I'm still working on letting go of. In the fourth grade, my class took a trip to the local university for a science day. We split into teams and rotated between three stations doing different experiments. One of the labs was to dissect a baby squid and learn about the anatomy of, well, squids.

The morning went pretty well and by lunch we were all back at school. Class resumed after lunch and my elementary school had hooks in the hallway for our backpacks. So about an hour later there was a funny smell coming from the row of backpacks in the hallway. My teacher deduced that it was coming from my backpack, and upon further investigation, there was a rotting baby squid tucked away in there.

Later I discovered it was my bully who put it there as a joke, but I endured the teacher's yelling in the hallway, with four classes in view, other kids laughing, as if I took the squid back myself. I had to put my backpack outside and I was so mortified, so ashamed, that I left school without it at the end of the day.

I eventually went back and got it after the sun went down. I secretly hoped it wasn't there. I don't remember having to explain it to my parents. I think I threw it away in the trash can and used a different bag. Maybe I said I lost my backpack to avoid more shame at home. I did stand my ground and say I didn't do it at the time. It wasn't my fault my teacher didn't believe me. It wasn't my fault someone thought about doing that kind of thing to a nine-year-old.

When looking back on the past, there might be some memories that really suck. Memories you wish would never happen again. Things happen. As a child I didn't understand that I could just let it go, that whatever others did to me really had nothing to do with me. Yes I was pretty embarrassed. But that is in the past. I now have the choice to laugh it off, thank the situation for showing me something about myself, and let it go.

So, what are you remembering now?

REGRET

Unless you are clairvoyant, no one really knows what will happen in every moment. So when things happen why do we feel regret? We like to think: 'I should have done this or that.' But there is nothing to be done about it. And we often feel regret for ourselves, and throughout our lives, especially when other people are involved.

As the saying goes, hindsight is 20/20. If you believe that everything happens for a reason, and are appreciative for life as it is, then there would be no need for regret.

As humans, we like to play the "what if" game. What if I never met that person? What if I married someone else? What if I learned to play soccer instead of football? What if this. What if that. We have many choices in life, and picking one path over another can cause regret to surface at a later moment in time. So, how do we let go of regret? By remembering that every decision we make is absolutely perfect. Every decision is just an experience.

Ok, so you can't go back and change the past and live a new life this time around. So why regret it? The life you are living in this moment is what matters. If you want to change it from here on out, go for it. But there is no crawling back to the past. The path changed as soon as you made the decision.

Now, I would like to share two personal stories of regret.

Understanding regret helps with letting go of it. Some things happen outside our realm of control. We can choose to feel regret for the rest of our lives, and we can make conscious decisions to prevent thoughts of regret in future moments. Regret is just another choice. It can be dealt with both before and after a situation happens.

<u>Ollie's Story</u>

Ollie was a cat who lived for only four years. My family had cats growing up, and I have always considered myself a cat lover, so when I moved out of my parent's house Ollie was my new cat. My other cats were still alive and well, over a decade old living a good life with my mom and dad, and I never experienced any problems with them as a child. Within three years of adopting Ollie he developed crystals in his bladder and had a few UTIs. My partner and I spent thousands of dollars in surgery to remove the blocks in his urinary tract because he could no longer go to the litter box.

He was never the same after surgery. He developed serious mood swings and we even tried medication. One cat-sized dose of an anti-psychotic turned Ollie into a zombie. That broke my heart. I threw out the rest of the medication but it didn't really matter. We made the decision to put Ollie down just a few days later when the crystals blocked him from using the litter box for good.

I blamed myself for Ollie's death, and the life leading up to his death. I felt really bad about trying the medication. I felt like I failed him. Apparently male cats, especially those who don't naturally drink a lot of water, need more water in their diet. Ollie was on a dry food only diet for three years. I blamed myself for not knowing that kind of thing in advance. My other male cats growing up were all on dry food only diets. But I guess they drank water like fishes. Ollie did not.

I went through hell with Ollie. It brought up all the things I thought I did wrong. We don't understand a lot of things until afterwards. We're not given the whole picture of our own lives, let alone the lives of others. With Ollie, things were out of my realm of control. So why do I feel regret? I attached a certain outcome, an expectation, and a responsibility to taking care of an animal. I felt like I failed both Ollie and myself. But why should I feel bad for not knowing something ahead of time?

The ego likes to give ourselves a hard time. I can let go of feeling any regret and guilt over Ollie's death by remembering that I loved him and that all I ever did for him came from love. It didn't work out the way I wanted it to, but Ollie had his own life to live. And that experience showed me what I needed to learn at the time.

My Tattoo Story

As a teenager I started to have the idea I'd get a tattoo when I was old enough. I thought it would be pretty cool to get a dragon tattooed on my back. But my eighteenth birthday came and went. My twenty-first birthday came and went. My twenty-seventh birthday came and went. I guess I kind of chickened out for a while. I liked to regret every year I never had the guts to get a tattoo as well. But 'lo and behold I finally did. And thankfully it was after I started to understand regret and use it to my advantage.

Nearing my twenty-eighth birthday, over a decade of wishing for a tattoo, I finally decided to go through with it. The dragon tattoo on the back didn't interest me anymore. I thought: what's the point in having a tattoo if you can't see it? Knowing nothing about tattoos, I walked in with the idea of getting a small outline of a cat and the word 'love' tattooed on my wrist. The tattoo artist politely told me that was not going to work as I had imagined it. So I panicked and left.

My boyfriend helped me flush out my ideas of the kind of tattoo I wanted that night and we went back the next day with a completed drawing: a black and white tuxedo cat and the word 'love' underneath, big enough to cover my forearm. I didn't sleep much that night. I had to get okay with everything that might mean in my life.

I made the conscious decision to get a tattoo first of all. Then I went through all the thoughts that surfaced with getting it on my forearm where everyone would be able to see it for the rest of my life. I had to ask myself if I could live with people staring, with people asking questions, with people judging me on my appearance, with not getting certain jobs or possibly having to cover up for others. I got okay with all of it. No compromises to expect. I wasn't going to be embarrassed for it. I wasn't going to regret it.

Now I was lucky enough to know this stuff before I decided on my tattoo. Regret is not fun to work with, but it can be worked with. You just have to get okay with it. You just have to get okay with whatever happened, wherever your life has lead you thus far, and that whatever happens now happens as it was meant to.

LOVE

"If you truly loved yourself, you could never hurt another."
-Buddha

True love is unconditional. True love is realizing that all you are is a being of pure love, and nothing less than such. If you don't love yourself in this moment, that's okay. You will. If you think mom, dad, grandma, grandpa or whoever raised you never loved you, that's okay too. Children aren't taught to love themselves because you can't love someone else until you love yourself.

Most of the kind of love we experience over our human lifespan is conditional love. We tend to love others if they only do this or only if they do that. True love is never abandoned or forgotten when things don't go our way, or when others are not who we think they are.

Unconditional love is loving everything just as it is. No expectations. No attachments.

Parents and caregivers love their children but often that love blinds them to how their love is being portrayed. We think we're doing the best for our children, our partners, our families, our pets. Even with the best intentions, we all perceive things differently. We infer emotions, we infer intention. And if actions are not explained or don't make sense then we have doubts.

Actions and words need to match in order to be understood and considered trustworthy. And love is a major source of trust issues when words and actions don't match up.

Telling others how to love you is conditional. Our needs change in every moment. One minute you may want to cuddle up on the couch with your partner, and the next you may want to be a thousand miles away from them. Whatever it is, it doesn't mean they stopped loving you. It doesn't mean you stop loving someone else. And if they do stop loving you, or you stop loving them, then it wasn't true love in the first place. Trust in your own self-love because that is all that matters.

Everyone has something in their lives to show them unconditional love until they can find it within themselves. It could be a family pet like a cat or a dog, a relative, and even a stranger during a chance encounter. Unconditional love is the goal of life, the essence of life. Choose love every time. If you come from a place of love and honor, others will respect you because you respect and love yourself.

If you are having a hard time loving yourself, start telling yourself that you love you. Say it at least once a day, every day. And keep saying it until you believe it. Every glance in the mirror say: 'I love you.' Say it over and over again. The only person who can love you is you.

Everyone is worthy of love. *You* are worthy of love. Love yourself and expect others to love themselves before loving you.

Relationships

Let's redefine a relationship. Let's expect others to love themselves before loving us. Let's expect to love ourselves before we can love another. Communicating honestly is the key. Many people don't love themselves. They were never shown how to, never told it was possible, never believed they were loved before. Love is a choice. I keep repeating that word…choice. Believe you have that choice.

As I said before, our needs change in every moment. That means other people's needs change in every moment as well. We can't expect others to look at our ass and read our minds. Humans change their mind all the time. We've been told this kind of behavior is indecisive or that we're 'all over the place.' But this is who we are. We have needs that fluctuate, needs that flow in the direction of every new moment like water down a river. It can be harder to deal with this fact in any kind of relationship, because what you do usually affects your family, friends, and partners. But it doesn't have to.

Relationships are not set in stone. There is no such thing as a "good" parent, a "good" wife, a "good" husband, a "good" child, or a "good" friend. Good and bad are just perceptions. Our roles change as we change. It is perfectly okay if your needs grow beyond the needs of your family's, friend's and partner's. Express yourself as you are. Find like-minded people. There is no need to act or pretend just to keep a relationship from changing, or from ending.

Family

Family is what you make it. What does having a family mean to you? How does this differ from your actual experiences with family? What we think family "should be" verses our own personal reality often doesn't match up. Why?

The entire thought of a family, the belief system of the family, or the very concept of family, is just another story. Whether it's a mom and a dad with two kids and a dog, or two moms or two dads or single parents or no parents at all...we all have our own family story. And from all the stories of all the families throughout history, we form new definitions of what family means to us. And that definition can change in every moment.

Now, sometimes you have to walk away from people. And not just literally walk away from them, but mentally distance yourself too. If it is in your best interest then there is nothing wrong with it. But when it comes to family, this decision can either be an easy one or a hard one.

If anything but love is what you are experiencing from someone, anyone, then that person doesn't need to continue to affect your life. Living in the now is about living and experiencing love in every moment. I've had to distance myself from people in my life, family included, because what I need is important too. I've made new friends, new family. And you can too, if you need to.

Friends

As children, we have a limited pool of options for family and friends. Often who lives in our neighborhood, who we go to school with, and who we see at church or the rec center, among other places, make up our general pool of potential friendships.

And if you moved around a lot as a child friendship might have been ever harder to come by.

As adults, we tend to find people who are more like-minded and have similar interests. Besides the internet, adults tend to move around for higher education or work options. The pool widens and more options become available as we grow older.

Regardless of how many friends we had as a child, or how many friends we have as an adult, the fact is that friendships come and go. We change. We grow apart. And there is nothing wrong with that. By the end of high school I had several friends; we all exchanged information, swearing we would always be friends. I haven't talked to a single one of them in over ten years. The same thing happened with the new friends I made in college. When we went our separate ways, we developed our own stories without each other. I stay in contact with four people from all of years of schooling and work. I've moved around a lot.

So don't give yourself a hard time for growing apart from the people you grew up with. Don't give your friends a hard time for growing in the direction they need to as well, even if that means growing apart from you and your story.

Intimate Relationships

Loving yourself before loving another applies to intimate relationships as well. They say love is not the same as sex, but then why are we so obsessed with it as a society?

Sexual relationships can be seen as seeking validation or self-worth from another person. And when this validation isn't received, one can feel a wide range of emotions, from shame and sadness to anger and guilt. My partner and I stopped having sex for a few years. We stayed together because we loved each other, but we also realized that we really didn't really love ourselves. I hated my body and was very self-conscious. I didn't want to have sex with me, so why would I expect anyone else to.

If you and your partner both loved yourselves, neither would seek love from the other. Relationships should mean something beyond just sex. The image, the idea, of sex is practically everywhere we look. It's easy to let others tell us how we're supposed to act. We're fascinated with gossip about other people's relationships because we want to feel better about ourselves and our own relationship situation.

But if we keep looking elsewhere we will never be happy. Happiness is realizing you have everything you already need. There is no need to keep searching for it in another person. Find the love within yourself and your relationships will show more love in return.

THANK YOU

'Thank you' is one of the most powerful word combinations, second only to 'I love you.' Letting go of the past is a continuous process, for each day is a new day and each yesterday can be let go of.

Practice gratitude and appreciation in every moment. Your past has made you the person you are today. Those experiences shaped your world. Be grateful for all your emotions, they showed you what you needed to be worked on. Be grateful for all your experiences, for they give excitement to life. And be grateful for their release as well.

Emotions are just experiences. It's good to have them. You have fear, anger, sadness, guilt, regret, etc. The point is not to get stuck in them. New moments mean new experiences. You just have to let go of the way you experienced something in the past. No two experiences are identical. They may be similar, but there is always something different and new about them.

If you're thinking you're stuck in the same old thing over and over again, then you need to make the choice on whether or not to get yourself un-stuck. So anger (or whichever emotion) keeps coming up, so what? Say thank you but you are no longer necessary. Say thank you to yourself. Thank you for being who you are.

Living in the now means being grateful in every moment. Notice a beautiful sunrise? Say thank you. Is it a cloud-less night where you can see the stars? Say thank you. The local bakery had your favorite muffin in stock? You know where I'm going with this. See everything as a gift, a gift to be thankful for, and the universe will provide more gifts. You just have to look for them.

SO LONG TOMORROW

WORRY

Worry is just a future thought. And most of those thoughts will never actually manifest in your reality. Now there is a difference between thinking and dreaming. Our thoughts tend to run amok, especially when the ego is involved, and we think bad things will happen if we do this or that.

Worrying keeps us in survival mode. Worrying prevents us from trying new things or expecting different results when we try things again. Everything in life is an experience. If you can believe that nothing happens that isn't supposed to happen, then there would be no need to worry about the future.

Humans worry about a lot of things. Besides worrying about our survival, we tend to let our imagination run wild thinking of scenarios where people won't like what we wear, how we talk or how we act, what we drive to work, if the store will have our brand of coffee in stock, if we're going to be sick, etc. etc.

There is a kind of freedom in not caring about what other people think. There is a kind of freedom in not constantly worrying about things that will never happen. Past experiences dictate perceptions of the future, but, if you look closely at your thoughts, you'll realize how ridiculous and unwarranted your worries are.

The Art of Overthinking

Worrying is truly an art form. Taking a thought and twisting it so out of proportion that it consumes your every thought, dream, and action is art. Overthinking can ruin a moment. Overthinking makes things appear worse than they actually are.

When humans get nervous, when fear starts to creep into their thoughts, worrying is expecting the worst case scenario. Use this expectation to your advantage in overcoming your thought trains. Expect that everything is perfect. Expect that everything will be okay.

Do you consider yourself a planner? I used to plan every moment of every day. I always had a to-do list. I always had something in the works, whether it was a project for school, something for work, a new craft idea, or the next video game adventure. Yes, I strategized my way through virtual and real life alike. Obviously this is not living in the present moment.

Giving up a little control in your life is difficult for a lot of people. Living in the moment, no plans, no expectations, can appear unrealistic at times. There has to be some leeway because we are still living in a world where things are not instantaneous.

Say it is dinner time and you want chili, the home-made kind that takes hours to cook. You are doing your best to live in the moment but it's kind of hard to have home-made chili that you just thought about a second ago.

So a little foresight is expected and helps with decisions in the moment. Just don't be concerned about the details. You may decide to make that chili, let it simmer all day, and then decide you wanted a pizza instead. Don't give yourself a hard time about it. You are allowed to change your mind.

The "What If" Game

When our human minds run amok, we often think a lot of "what ifs." What if I lose my job today? What if it rains tomorrow and ruins the hike I planned? What if the car doesn't start? What if the bus is late? What if my pants rip in public? You get the idea...

Use the "what if" game to your advantage. Use it to let go of the past. Use it to let go of attachments to the future. Overcome your fears by accepting all possibilities in life and expecting the positive ones to actually happen.

Remember positive and negative are just perceptions. What if something awesome happens? What if that change is for the best? What if I was meant to stay inside and curl up with a book today? What if losing that job was the best thing that ever happened to me?

Worrywarts often drive themselves, and those around them, crazy. If you want change in your life, then go for it. But let the little details fall into place on their own.

Use your imagination positively and not for worrying about the details of future moments you have no control over. You decide which thoughts you want to keep thinking in every moment. You can continue to worry, or you can let your worries go and replace them with new thoughts.

FEAR

Fear is an illusion. Fear is just a perception. It isn't really real. Fear can be seen as an emotion fueled by a belief system. Many thoughts make up fear. And fear isn't always about something bad happening, although that is what usually comes to mind first. What you may not realize is that we often fear "good" things happening to us as well. We can fear success and we can fear love. Look at your fears and see the themes.

We often fear feeling certain emotions. All of the emotions we have every felt, or have ever heard of being felt, can cause fear to surface throughout our lives. Why? No one really wants to live in anger, guilt, depression, or shame, especially for long periods or forever. No one wants to be in pain, emotional, mental or physical.

We all want to be happy. We all want to be free. It's the fear of happiness that can keep us stuck in life. What if I do that and I'm not happy? So what? Get happy about it, or do something else.

Every time you think: "I can't do that," ask yourself why. Is it fear? Is it something, a thought, someone told you to believe? And why do you believe it. Your answer could very well be a rational explanation, and then it could be entirely ridiculous. Go with what your heart says.

Fear is a choice we make. Make it consciously from now on. Don't let your automatic programs and thoughts continue to run your world. There is fear, and then there is worrying that your fears will come true. Fears will continue to surface in new experiences, but you have the ultimate choice to let them control how you live your life.

Defense Mechanisms

Fear exposes our defense mechanisms. Fear exposes our auto-responses when we feel scared or threatened in some way. What happens when someone cuts you off in traffic? How do you react?

My first response is something to the effect that that guy was an asshole. But what makes him an asshole? I know nothing about that guy and whether or not he cut me off intentionally. So why care so much about it? Because my ego felt threatened. That guy should know how to drive better. That guy should have left earlier if the reason he cut me off was because he was late.

These are just thoughts we tell ourselves to feel better. All my fears of being in an accident surfaced in that incident, and my first response was to call some random person names and get angry. See what your automatic responses are when your fears are exposed.

Overcoming Fear

Sometimes, in order to overcome our fears, we have to do the things we fear the most.

Afraid of spiders? Go hold a tarantula.
Afraid of the dark? Go without a nightlight in a trusted place.
Afraid of what you might look like without hair? Shave it off.

And then some fears are more complicated and need to be dealt with on another level, mentally. Listen to your thoughts. Listen to your fears. Why are you afraid of that?

If you are afraid to go to the movies or out to dinner by yourself because of what people might think of you, then you might want to consider doing just that. Who cares what other people think? Apparently you do. And if you don't want to care about other people's perception of you, then do things that will help boost your own confidence.

I am still working on overcoming this type of fear. When I have a thought that I shouldn't wear that or go do something because of what someone else might think, I stop and ask myself why not. If it's just a crazy thought I laugh it off. But if I can't get over thinking that wearing my comfy pants out to lunch is somehow offensive to strangers who will never see me again, then I march myself to lunch in my comfy pants and silently freak out until I can laugh about it later.

Do what you are comfortable with in overcoming your fears. Spiders freak me out, and I have certainly not worked up to holding a tarantula yet. But I am comfortable getting a tattoo on my arm as one way to stop caring about what other people think of me.

I overcome my fear of failure by accomplishing something small each and every day. And when this book is published, I will have done something to stand up to both my fear of failure and my fear of success. Maybe no one will ever read this sentence. Maybe more people than I can imagine will read this sentence. No worries either way.

See what thoughts your fears trigger within you. Question your fears. Figure out how valid they truly are. Believing your fears is a choice. Ask yourself: "What's the worst that can happen?"

WHAT'S THE WORST THAT CAN HAPPEN?

Steps for Overcoming Fear and Worries about the Future:

1. Ask: What's the worst that can happen?
2. Think: How realistic is it?
3. Get okay with that thing happening

This is one exercise you want to let your imagination run wild. Think of a scenario with one of your fears and ask: what is the worst that can happen?

Listen to all the thoughts that come up. See all the possible outcomes to your fear. Make a list. Then when the list is done, go over it and see if you can get okay with every single thing happening, as if it would happen for real. When you can get okay with everything you can think of, you will no longer be afraid.

So, how realistic are your fears? Look at your list and see how many outcomes are actually possible. Most fears are irrational, ridiculous even. You'll scratch a lot of things off your list that are highly unlikely to ever happen. Then it is time to get okay with everything else.

How do you get okay? Well that is up to you. Can you live with losing your job? Losing a friend? Embarrassing yourself in public? Dying?

Why can't you get okay with something happening? Is it more fear? Work with every thought that comes up. Break down your fears until they no longer make sense, then see how real they truly are.

Remember it is a continuous process. Different situations bring up different fears and combinations of fear. You'll have the same fear resurface over and over again until you've worked through all possible outcomes and scenarios; until you no longer believe it, and until it is no longer a fear.

What do you fear? What is holding you back from achieving your dreams? What is holding you back from being happy? Face the fear and it will go away. Invalidate your worries about a tomorrow that will never happen.

A saying that also helped me in overcoming my fears is: "I recognize the fear and move past it." Find what works for you. Break down your thoughts and start believing that your fears do not really exist.

JUDGMENT

Judgment has a bad reputation. Many people fear the so-called Judgment Day because they fear they will be judged for their perceived sins. No one likes to be judged. In fact, many fears derive from the fear of judgment. If you think you live a life without judgment, think again. We all judge, but mostly we don't realize it. Until now.

Here is a simple way to look at it: Opinion = Judgment.

If you have an opinion about something, you are in fact judging it. Some judgment is obvious, but most of the time it is subtle. Our subtle judgments shine a light on the underlying thoughts about ourselves and our lives. Little comments, opinions, about daily things tell us how we think and what we think. Opinions tell us where our expectations are. "Normal" is a false perception in our minds about how things "should" be.

When you think about your daily routine, what are you thinking about? Is it a nice day out? Is it too cloudy for you?

Maybe you didn't like the shade of red that car was when it passed you on the street. Or that the trashcan was too full in the mall food court for your liking. Every little opinion equates to some underlying judgment. Perhaps you would have chosen a different shade of red if you had that car. And maybe someone wasn't doing their job well enough if the trashcan was almost full.

Why do you think the things you do? Why do you say the things you do? Only you can answer these questions to find what you are really saying about yourself.

Worrying about Judgment

Why are you worried about what someone else is thinking? Are you worried you did something wrong? Said the wrong thing? We even judge ourselves when we do the right thing. What if wasn't really right? Why do you care about all these things? That's not an easy question to answer.

Not fearing judgment is a hard thing to do. You can't stop worrying, you can't let go of the fear, until you figure out why you think the way you do. When we judge something, what we are really doing is judging ourselves. Everybody is judging their journey right now. You have to be okay with whatever it is you are experiencing. Don't judge it.

In the end, people will judge you anyway. You can live your life impressing others or you can live your life impressing yourself. Just be yourself, albeit this is one of the hardest things we have to learn to do. Some days I am really good at not worrying about other people's judgment. And other days I don't say what I want to say, or eat what I want to eat, because of the people I am with.

All we can do is work with our thoughts, really hear what we are saying, and decide if we want to continue to think that way in every moment.

FEAR OF REJECTION

Many fears branch out from the fear of judgment. Rejection is one of those fears. It affects how we love, how we think, what we have and what we don't have. We fear being rejected for what we drive, what clothes we wear, how we style our hair. We either dress to impress or dress to avoid.

Ask yourself if you are doing things for yourself or for another person. Ask yourself why you're not wearing that dress or that tie to the party. Maybe your partner dislikes the way you dress, or maybe you're hoping to make a good first impression. Why do we let others influence and intimidate our decisions? Fear; plain and simple. We want to be accepted. But what we really want is to be loved.

The secret to overcoming the fear of rejection is realizing that everybody else is too concerned and focused about their own selves to really care about what you're wearing or how your body looks. And if they have an opinion about you, then they are really having an opinion about themselves. Remember: opinion = judgment. We're all just judging ourselves.

We all experience embarrassment at one point or another. Throughout grade school I had shown on more than one occasion that my cheeks can turn quite the bright shade of red, even for the tiniest of incidents. We let others judgments affect us on a personal level. We let others make us feel like we do things wrong, that we *are* wrong. There is nothing wrong with being the real you. We are really just afraid of our own rejection. If you don't like yourself, then how do you expect anyone else to? If you're not comfortable being yourself when you are by yourself, why would you be comfortable around another person?

Don't live your life according to what others think. No matter what you do, or do not do, others will think of you as they think of themselves. People are going to laugh at you. People will call you names. So what if they don't like you? Who cares? Is that really your problem? There are billions of people in the world, and most of them are connected by the internet. Find someone who does like you for who you are. There are more people like that out there than you may think.

FEAR OF LOSING CONTROL

The truth is you have both no control and absolute control over your life. What do I mean by this? You may not be able to control someone's negative behavior, but you can control how you respond to it. You can control how long you participate in it. You can control what you believe and what you think.

Control is really just an illusion. Fear of losing control can prevent someone from living life to the fullest. We tend to hang on to things that we can sense, things that are tangible. What we fear most is not being able to control the things we can't see.

We tend to get emotional about not feeling in control. The ego likes to be in control. And the ego will make it seem like *you* are in control, but that is the illusion. Learning how to be in control of your own life can be scary and emotional. One can experience anger, sadness, and joy, among many other emotions, when they realize how much actual control they have in their life. Whether you felt in-control or out-of-control in the past, you can be in control in this moment.

So if you can't control the universe, and you can't control others, then why be afraid of losing control? Remember that you have sole responsibility over one thing, and that is you: your reactions to thoughts and emotions, the words spoken to yourself and others, and how you choose to live your life in every moment. That is your control. And you can never lose that.

Control Issues

Are you someone who needs things to be done "their" way? Do you think that your way is the 'right' way? People with control issues, and I am pointing the finger towards myself as well, insist on others doing things their way.

Now, your way may not make sense to others. And your way may not even be practical for them. The way they need to do something may be entirely different than yours. Respect other people's needs as well as your own.

We can also be too protective when interjecting our opinions into other people's experiences. We think we're helping, but we may actually be imposing on another person's journey. It's okay to let others make 'mistakes'. You may be able to provide a little advice or share your stories, but they are free to choose something different.

We are all different. We are all on our own journey. We can't even protect ourselves from learning life's lessons and experiences. So why do we think we can shield someone else from their journey?

Power

We often equate control with power. And it is the loss of power, or the perception of that loss, that is one of the main fears people have. This may not seem obvious at first. Do you feel powerless in any aspect of your life? How about at work, school or in general? Usually if someone feels powerless, they feel like they have no control over their life or the situation.

What we do have is absolute power over our personal actions and reactions. We can never lose that. We are responsible for our own thoughts. No one has power over another person, place, or thing, including the universe. We think we do, but we don't. Our responsibility is to our own story, and we can only control so much of it. We have to let go of the parts we can't control.

We give away our power to other people and things all the time. We let people affect us on an emotional level. We can become dependent on outside forces to make us happy, or to show us love.

Happiness can only come from within. If you're only happy when you're with someone, or doing something, then you are not really happy. Be responsible for your happiness in any situation. Be responsible for expecting love from yourself first. Find the strength within to realize your own power, your own worth, and take control of your story.

FEAR OF FAILURE

There is no such thing as failure. The perception of failure is all in your head. Failure is taught by society, in the school system, in the workplace. The fear of failure keeps us from trying new things, from trying things more than one time, and from trying things in a different way. We tend to do the same things over and over again because we think it is safe. The reason why many people give up so quickly is because they look at how far they still have to go instead of realizing how far they've come. Everything is a success if we're experiencing something and learning from it.

Mistakes are the main source of feeling like a failure. Trust that mistakes are okay. They are just an experience. We are meant to have many experiences and learn from many mistakes throughout our lifetimes. We tend to throw parents and other caregivers under the bus when they make mistakes especially. No one is perfect. Plenty of parents drop their newborn children. Plenty of parents forget to pick up their kids from school. Don't take it personal.

But let's say they admit they did it on purpose, then what? It really had nothing to do with you and everything to do with them, so why let it continue to bother you? Everyone makes mistakes. Honor their mistakes. Honor your mistakes.

There is also no such thing as failing to complete a project.

Human beings are not meant to finish everything. If we're living in the now, then all we have are moment to moment projects. We think we have to finish what we start though. We think we have to accomplish everything we set out to do. Nope. Starting and not finishing a project is an experience all to itself. We learn something new, and when we're done with that experience we move on to the next one. Don't give yourself a hard time about it.

We spend a lot of money, time, and energy on crafts, hobbies, skills...anything that is creative and fun. It's ok not to be into it after you try something. It's ok to move onto the next thing you're dreaming about. Some things you'll find you are truly passionate about and you'll want to keep experiencing over and over again, and other times not so much.

Perfection

Perfectionism is learned from society and our caregivers primarily. Have you ever been told to 'be the best that you can be'? What we really expect is perfection: straight A's in school, top scores on tests, winners in sports and in life, because that is what our parents were graded on, how they based their worth growing up as a child themselves and then as an adult. Perfection is subjective. Being 'good enough' can be either first place or just giving it a try.

We fear not being good enough for others, and for ourselves, because our self-worth has been tied up with others' perceptions of worthiness. We think we have to do this or that in order to be worthy; worthy of love, affection, respect. There is no such thing as perfection and there is also only perfection within everything. True perfection is imperfection. Everything is perfect just as it is. *You* are perfect just as you are.

Don't wait for the perfect moment, there is no such thing. The ego likes perfection, or the idea of it, to keep you in any moment other than this one. It keeps you judging this moment as something it is not. There are limitless possibilities to everything, so nothing will ever be perfect if you keep waiting for it to be. Perfection is unobtainable because you already have it. So, where are you holding out for things to be perfect?

Fear of Lack

Lack can be seen as a failure involving money or material things. If attachment is the root of all suffering, then money is certainly one of the biggest attachments mankind can have. Some people are so afraid of lack that they never have enough, even if they have everything. They are also not happy with what they have either.

Instead of feeling less than, based on numbers in your bank account or pieces of paper in your wallet, exchange the money you do have for opportunity: the opportunity to experience something on your journey, whether it is buying a guitar to learn to play, a trip around the world, a new pair of shoes, or even a sandwich to get you through the day.

Be conscious of the intention you have involving money. Be okay with accepting a gift. There is no need to drag pride into the mix with thinking about charity. Support your journey, consciously. Support other's journeys where you can. Accept support from others as well. Sharing can be scary. Change your thoughts about what it means to have, what it means to give and what it means to receive.

FEAR OF PAIN

As discussed previously, emotional pain is often worse than physical pain. However, it is the physical pain we fear the most. We often don't realize how much emotional pain we are in until we can't ignore it anymore.

Ultimately pain is just a perception. The human mind and body have been shown to push beyond physical pain at times and it's also good at suppressing both mental and emotional pain.

Human beings tend to not like pain. We do whatever we can to avoid it. We live as if no one can hurt us by putting up walls. We push others away to avoid the pain of rejection and loss. We mentally distance ourselves from people and situations we fear will cause pain as well. But pain is unavoidable. The human ego gets bruised. The ego gets hurt.

Pain doesn't actually last forever. We've told ourselves it does. We hold onto pain to feel something, anything, especially if we can't believe in feeling anything else. Pain is a belief, a mindset. It doesn't feel like it but it is.

Some people even believe they deserve pain as some sort of punishment or retribution for their guilt or regret. No one deserves pain; not for the past and not in the future. Escaping our perceptions of pain can become an addiction. Fearing pain can keep us stuck in a moment and keep us from experiencing that moment to the fullest.

Have you ever had someone tell you something was going to hurt and so you were afraid to do it? But then one day you do and you realize it didn't hurt at all. Like getting my tattoo; I had it built up in my head that it was going to hurt beyond what I might be able to handle. But it turned out to be a different kind of pain, not what I expected at all, and I even laughed at myself for thinking I wouldn't be able to handle it. Figure out what you are afraid of feeling. Do you avoid situations where you might get hurt?

Our pain is our own. You can't compare yourself, your life or your pain, to others. Remember that everything is relative and subjective. No one can tell you that what you are feeling doesn't hurt. And you can't tell anybody else how much pain they should or should not be in. Your agony is your own. Your misery is no more painful than another's. It's our egos that think so and turn pain into a competition.

Whether we're in physical or emotional pain, adding more emotional pain on top by suggesting we are wrong for feeling that way isn't the solution. When you think of stubbing your toe, what hurts worse? The ten seconds of physical pain, or the thinking that you are stupid for stubbing your toe in the first place? Work with your thoughts to understand your own pain while giving yourself permission to feel the way you do, as well as permission to let go of that pain.

Abuse

Emotional abuse, just like emotional pain, is often worse than physical abuse. Emotional abuse is harder to realize as well. It often isn't until an abusive interaction or relationship turns physical that one realizes they were being abused at all. The human mind is a powerful thing, and it can believe anything it wants to. Over time, emotional abuse can become the norm. It can become self-destructive when we start to believe the things other people tell us, and their words become our own. Have you ever been told you are worthless? Have you ever felt worthless?

When one can't handle their pain, they may look to release that energy elsewhere. This release can either be self-destructive or destructive towards another, both emotionally and physically. Often people use emotional pain against another. When people are hurt, when people are in pain, they can use that pain as an excuse to hurt another. We can lash out physically from emotional pain and anger. But this kind of energetic release turns into an abusive cycle.

It is just as easy to release one's emotional pain by one's self, without having to resort to hurting another. Whether one has been abused or abusive, abuse often stems from feelings of unworthiness, fear, anger, and blame. Realize what kind of pain you are in. Listen to the words you tell yourself. Listen to the words you tell others. Words are powerful. The human mind believes things easier when they are told things over and over again. Everyone has pain. You alone can deal with your pain. There is no need to add more pain to anyone's story, including your own.

FEAR OF LOSS

Loss reminds us of our own mortality, our own inevitable death to which we have little to no control over. Many emotions, many thoughts, compose the memories and attachments we have to those we have lost, and those we fear to lose. The fear of loss can make us hold on so tight that we suffocate without realizing it. And that fear can make us fight when letting go. No one wants to lose.

One way of looking at it is that there is no such thing as loss; we just gain something we were not aware of before. It is our reactions to the losses and gains in our lives that define the story, that define the moment. Sometimes people leave us. Sometimes we leave other people. The loss of life, or the perceived loss of life, is usually not considered a happy thing. Loss can be both a happy moment and a sad moment.

With relationships, fear of loss keeps us holding on. We have the 'blood is thick than water' and 'we've got to stick together' mentalities when it comes to family. This makes the pain and the fear worse when those ties are broken.

One might feel like they can't go on without somebody, especially a spouse. That they can't forget and they can't forgive. Can't, or won't? These are just thoughts. Why can't you move on? Why won't you forget? What *can* you do about it?

This goes back to feeling powerless to a thought. Loss can make us feel powerless. Loss reminds us that we can't control everything in the universe.

It's okay to remember those we've lost. It's okay to forget them too. Just don't let your thoughts weigh you down, keeping you from growing and expanding beyond your loss. Be aware of your thoughts. The pain can go away. There is no need to hold onto guilt and regret. Your well-being is just as important. Detach all but love from that memory of the person, animal, or thing that you have lost or fear to lose. Until all but love remains within your thoughts, and your heart, you will find it hard to experience living in the now to the fullest.

So, what do you fear losing? Where are your attachments? Can you get okay with losing that thing? Loss can bring up a myriad of fears. Loss can bring up questions you may not want to answer. You can choose to move beyond loss, and you can choose to let it consume you.

FEAR OF BEING ALONE

Sometimes people leave us. But that does not mean we are alone. Children grow up and leave home in search of a new one. Everyone grows. Everyone leaves at some point. But you are never truly alone, ever, whether someone has left you or you are doing the leaving.

Loneliness is a thought, a perception, an expectation to have others around us, and an attachment to relying on outside sources for guidance. No one is an island. Humanity is linked. Being comfortable being alone and being lonely are too different things. There is always someone to talk to. There is always someone who cares about you, even if that person is yourself. How does that differ from being alone? It's all your perception. Even if you were all by yourself, with no one else around, you don't have to be lonely.

Loneliness is a choice. Yep, I keep saying that word; choice. You can still feel lonely in a crowd of people. So what does it matter if you are alone or not? It isn't dependent on the amount of people around you or how many people you think you can communicate with about your life.

Loneliness is all in the mind. The ego likes to keep us in a state of fear. We rely on others, or so we're told to do so. We rely on being in the presence of others to solve our problems, or to validate our existence. The secret is that we already have everything we need in life. Everything else is just an experience.

Become your own best friend. Love what you do. Love who you are. Love what makes you happy and passionate about life. Whether you are in a crowd or the only one in the room, you can choose to be lonely or not. Learn to enjoy your own company. The problem with loneliness is that we usually can't stand to be alone with ourselves. We can't stand to be alone with our thoughts.

Alone Time

The fear of being alone can also be seen as the fear of facing ourselves. Being alone forces us to deal with our thoughts, our beliefs, and our perceived problems head on. We may not like what we see (i.e. self-judgment). As we grow up, we become more and more what others want us to be or what we think others want us to be. Who we really are, behind and underneath all the thoughts, beliefs, judgments, expectations, attachments and illusions, is what we are really afraid of. Who are you?

This may be one fear you need to work on first. You have to face yourself: your past, your fears of the future, and learn to deal with you. Isn't it easier to be told who to be? Push past the uneasiness of discovering who you truly are and you may actually like what you find. Realize what is true and what is false about you. Who do you really want to be?

Facing things alone can be easy and it can be difficult. Learning to trust ourselves; our judgment and our intuition, can be difficult at first. Our beliefs and thoughts are often tested most when we're on our own. When we have no one to compare ourselves to, when we only have our own thoughts for company, that is when we discover who we truly are.

So being alone isn't necessarily a bad thing. In fact, it's kind of a necessity. We all need alone time to figure out who we are, to learn how to trust ourselves, to discover what makes us happy, and to realize we don't need to search for validation from others. You can do this in the company of others; I'm not saying you have to go out and be by yourself for the rest of your life. Just honor the time you need to figure out your story.

FEAR OF THE UNKNOWN

The unknown: the literal and metaphorical dark. We fear the dark because it represents the unknown, while light represents what we do know. We shine a light on things when we are paying attention to them. When we are in the dark we don't know anything; we're left out of the loop.

The fear of the unknown is why we fear other people, why we fear situations, and why we fear the future. This fear encompasses all other fears and phobias. The ego likes knowing stuff. That is how it keeps us 'safe.' The ego equates knowledge to life, so the unknown must equal death. Fearing the unknown is a survival mechanism. The unknown may bring us pain, it may bring us loneliness, it might bring us failure…it fears all by jumping to conclusions. The unknown may very well be a pleasant experience, but we don't like to risk it.

We have been conditioned to fear the unknown. We've been told that what is known is safe. The unknown is dangerous territory. But that is just a story we tell ourselves. So what is the worst that can happen? What will you find in the dark? And why are you afraid?

<u>Change</u>

The fear of change can arguably be the root of the fear of the unknown. We like safe. We do things out of safe to protect our perceptions of the future. We may or may not realize this fear keeps us paralyzed to new opportunities. Change can be positive, if you let it. Change can bring new experiences you could never have imagined before. But change isn't easy. We fight to hold on and we fight to let go. Being aware of this fight will help you end it. How can you change what you don't know?

We fear what change will bring. Each and every moment is an unknown. Anything can happen. Everything is possible. We can't change the past. We can't change what we've set in motion to happen in the future. We just have to ride the ride and watch our thoughts about it along the way. The ride can be a nightmare, or the ride can be magical. It is your choice.

Death

Death is the ultimate unknown. Why are we so concerned about the afterlife? We often forget about this life we're living, right now. No one knows what will happen for sure. It's what you believe will happen that matters. Do you think you are going to a 'better' place, or a not so better place? Will there be a heaven, fire and brimstone, or a whole lot of nothing? What does it matter anyway?

Maybe we wake up when we die. That would be the opposite of what we currently think. It certainly is a possibility. Imagine what it would be like to go to sleep and never wake up. Can you get okay with not waking up? Who's to say we're all awake right now? Maybe life is just a dream.

Some people fear death so much that they never truly live. What is living anyway? What defines a life? Many of us secretly hold off living. Maybe, just maybe, Death will leave us be or give us more 'time' if we have unfinished business to attend to. We stave off death as long as we can by keeping to what's safe, and not taking those perceived risks. We put ourselves into little safe boxes, where we think nothing can hurt us if only we would stay in the box. Well now it is time to think outside the box. It is time to live outside the box. If we put ourselves into that box, certainly we can get ourselves out of it.

Death is unavoidable: it is just part of the game, it is just the end of the ride, and it is just the end of the story.

THE WAITING GAME

So what are you waiting for? Are you holding out for a 'better' tomorrow? We get ourselves stuck between the past and the present when we choose not to let go of old thoughts, and when we choose to continue worrying about the future. Our fears keep us from grabbing ahold of the present and living life moment to moment. Make the most of the moment you are in now. If you want to do something, do it now, don't wait.

People wait for Friday. People wait for summer. People wait for someone to fall in love with them. People wait for sunshine before adventuring out. You can't hold onto "what if one day..." or "if only it was the right time..." There is no such thing as the right time. There is only now.

Procrastination is really just fear. And it is our fears that keep us stuck waiting on something else to push us over the edge, or waiting until time runs out. Our thoughts create our reality. So if you're always thinking of waiting; waiting on someone else or waiting for a miracle, then that is the energy you will get in return...endless waiting.

Living in waiting may seem safe, it may seem like you are in control, but everything will be waiting for you to deal with when the cycle is broken. Everything will come to the surface at once if you wait to deal with it all at a later moment.

So are you living your life or are you just waiting to die? Are you waiting for the life you had planned instead of living the life that is right in front of you? There is a difference between living and just going through the motions. Search your thoughts and figure out what you keep waiting for.

Expectations and Attachments

We get attached to believing in certain futures as if they were the only ways we could become happy, successful, loved, etc. There is expecting something to happen and then there is getting disappointed when things don't happen the way you expected it to. My life certainly turned out different than I expected it to.

The trick is not getting stuck in the details. We do this all the time though: "I'm not going to write a novel because it will never make billions of dollars," or "I'm not going to paint unless everyone loves it". Placing conditions on our moments create expectations and attachments. When these conditions are not met, we create emotions, thoughts, and beliefs that need to be worked through again and again.

I know people who spend twenty dollars a week on lottery tickets and never win. Life is about options, yes, but it is not about fixating on a certain outcome. That is expectation. With anything, learn all the options, all the possibilities. Play a little here and there. Just don't put all your eggs in one basket, so to speak. Be grateful for what you do have.

How many old clothes do you have lying around, waiting for them to fit again? I held onto a pair of jeans, several dresses and some blouses for seven years. I finally let them all go, donated them, and less than six months later I needed to buy smaller clothes. Now, I know what you are thinking. You're thinking; "see, you should have held onto those clothes." I firmly believe that if I had, I would still be waiting to fit into them. You have to let go. Be happy with who you are. Believe in your perfection in every moment. And if at the back of your mind you want to lose weight, learn to love yourself just as you are and trust that you will when you are ready.

Those skinny jeans, those button-up shirts that no longer button, only keep you stuck in the past and waiting for a future that'll never happen...at least not how your ego is imagining it and not in the way you are waiting for. Change your thoughts: "If the day comes when I need new pants, then that's great. If not, I am perfectly happy with the pants I currently fit into. Size is just a number after all. I'm not going to worry about it." No expectations. No attachments.

LIVING IN THE NOW

WHAT DOES IT MEAN TO LIVE IN THE NOW?

Conscious thought is being observant. Observe your mindset every morning when you wake up. Observe your mindset in every moment. Be mindful in every moment. Everything you do can be done with intention. Expectation and attachment creates expectant and attached energy. Gratitude creates gracious energy.

Pay attention to what moment you are in. Are you thinking back to the past or off in the future? Being present has its advantages. One is less likely to get hurt if they're present. An example would be chopping vegetables with a knife; I've almost cut off the tip of my pinky finger letting my thoughts wander while I made dinner once or twice.

However, just awareness alone isn't consciousness. Thinking doesn't necessarily mean believing. Expect things to change.

Don't get stuck thinking nothing will change. Don't give up if things aren't changing 'fast enough' for you. It's easy to just give up and let the world change for you...until you realize it isn't changing the way you want it to.

Observe your thoughts when they come up. Don't force yourself to listen all the time, that might drive you crazy. Give yourself a mental break when you need to. Go do something fun. And don't give yourself a hard time for anything you choose to do. Do what you feel in every moment.

It is easy to forget how awesome you are. It's easy to forget you're just living a story, riding the ride, playing the play. It is easy to remember as well. We're all on our own paths, even when walking side by side.

Respect other people's journeys by making decisions with the highest good in mind. Decisions should never be made *against* another, or yourself. You have a choice in every moment. And everything can change in the blink of an eye.

HOW TO LIVE IN THE NOW

You can't live in a new world if you keep holding onto the old one. You can't change your story if you don't work on editing it. Embrace the now in every way that you can. The trick is to be present in body, mind *and* heart. Learn to appreciate every experience. This can be hard to do at first. You may think: "why should I be grateful for that?" Be mindful of your thoughts when they come up. You'll learn to recognize the thoughts you hear over and over again, and you'll learn to choose what thoughts you want to continue having. It takes a lot of practice. And you can only get discouraged if you let yourself do so.

Things to do in every moment:

Thank everything

Say thank you to everything. Say thank you to your body, it's the vessel that allows you to experience this journey. Spend time with it. Listen to it. Nourish it with yummy foods. Thank the sun for shining as well as the rain for falling. Thank the person who pushed your buttons today. Thank everything you remember to.

Prioritize

Realize your priorities. If you want a major change in your life, it may be time to focus on yourself. *You* are your priority. Make a list of things you really want to do, both daily to-dos and more expansive or long-term goals.

Do things for yourself

Your journey is your own. Focus on you. This may seem impossible if you have a family, kids, or a lot of perceived responsibilities. Start with the little things. Set aside some time for yourself every day, even if it's just taking a five-minute breather from your daily tasks. Pretty soon you'll want to take more time for yourself. Always have your interests in mind. We like being caretakers, just remember that you are just as important.

Go out in nature

Soak up the sun, get your feet dirty, dance in the rain, play in the ocean, stomp around in the mud, and get your hands dirty. Build something. Create something. The choices are limitless. Expand your mind by trying new things. Go outside your comfort zone. Embrace a challenge.

Be present in what you do

Even if you are taking a five minute shower, try not to think about the twenty million things you have to do after the shower, or the twenty million things that happened before the shower. Be *in* the shower. Savor it as if it were your last.

Be conscious of what you are doing. Pretend to soak up the sun as if you were a vampire who had just been cured and hasn't seen the sun in over a century. Revel in it. Finger paint as if you just discovered what cool, wet paint feels like between your fingers. Don't concern yourself with the clean-up. Don't concern yourself with what happens next. That is a different moment.

Affirmations

Who do you want to be? Who do you think you are? Are you perfect, happy, or something less than that? Chances are whoever you currently think you are you are not truly that. Do you want to be happy? Really ask yourself. Do you truly believe you are beautiful, or is there doubt somewhere in your thoughts?

Daily affirmations are things you want to remember. Repeat what you want to believe. *I am beautiful. I am worthy. I am loved.* If you want to learn to cook, start saying you are an excellent cook. If you want to start training for a marathon, start saying you are strong, that you are a fast runner, you swim well, etc. Claim it as you work towards your goals.

Remember to keep it positive. Create reminders if needed. I made cardboard signs and put them around my house where I would see them. Some people use sticky notes on their bathroom mirror or their refrigerator, places one often visits on a daily basis.

If you are short on space or don't want to remember a bunch of stuff, simply write "I am love" to encompass everything that you are, or "Remember" as your reminder. When I saw the sign 'remember' on my wall that meant to remember how beautiful I was and how awesome I am. Do whatever works best for you.

One has to believe something inside and out loud. When words match action you get truth. Say it until you believe it. Think it until you believe it. Believe it until you live it.

Getting Okay With the Now

Nothing lasts forever. We are meant to move on to the next moment, the next experience. Learn to get okay with whatever situation you are in. Ride the ride. Play the play. Be present and enjoy the moment for what it is. No judgment. No attachments.

Be okay with what works, and when things don't work out too. If you don't like something, change it. If you can't change it, what can you do about it? Pay attention to your thoughts. Focus on what you do like instead of the thoughts you want to let go of. Choose which memories you want to hold onto. Let go of old perceptions of family and friends.

Everything changes, everybody grows at different rates. Don't give yourself a hard time when you feel stuck, or when you keep changing your mind about what you want. The now is the now.

CHOICE

Living in the now is a choice. We often forget we have choice. We forget how amazing life can be. We forget how amazing we are as human beings having an experience on planet Earth. It is perfectly acceptable to choose to not live in the now. It is entirely your choice. If there is one thing we should all remember though, is that we are free to make a new choice in any moment.

Choices are made in every moment whether you realize it or not. Most of the time it is our unconscious programming running in the background that affects the lives we live, making people feel as if they had no choice. There is always a choice to be made. We just have to become aware of it first.

In every moment we are given a decision. To live in the now, learn to choose consciously from your heart. Choose what thoughts you want to keep listening to. The human mind complicates things by not believing in the simplicity of choice. When things look too easy, we don't tend to trust it.

Trust In Your Choices

Other people may have good intentions in telling you what to do and how to do it. But only one person truly knows what is best for you. And that is you. Humans are meant to make mistakes. That is how we learn. We have to learn by living our own stories, and by doing things our way. We absorb so much advice in our lifetimes, some of which is helpful, and some of which is not. Choice has to come from within. What we call intuition, or 'gut feelings,' guides our decisions in every moment. This shows us what our hearts truly want out of life.

It is our choices that show us who we really are. Do you want to be someone different? Then choose different. It's really that simple. Although you may have to keep choosing what you want until it's no longer a conscious choice and it becomes a part of who you are. Ultimate choice is over own our thoughts. *No I don't want to think that anymore. No, I'm not thinking that anymore.* We have to put your mental foot down and focus on what we do want to think from now on, in every moment.

It is up to each and every one of us to choose happiness, to choose love. It doesn't matter if you think you were born a certain way, or raised to be someone you're not. You can choose to be different now. You can choose to do different now. It's your choice to let go or to hold on. The only person suffering from a grudge is the one holding it.

Don't wait on others to choose. That is their choice. Don't wait for others to change with you, to see things your way, or stay with you every step of your journey. They have their own journey to make choices for. No one can force change upon another, they have to be ready for and accept that change themselves. And their choices may be different than yours. People drift apart. People walk different paths and choose different paths at different times.

Make your choices with the highest good in mind. That is all you can ask of yourself and of others.

BEING OKAY WITH YOU

Others will see you according to the way they see themselves. Learn to be okay with the way *you* see yourself. You should be exactly as you need to be in every moment and be okay with it. If you need to cry, then cry. If you need to shout and stomp your feet, then go do it. Give yourself permission to be who you need to be, and to not care what others think of you.

People change and grow. Let go of the old versions of you. People change all the time. At the start of this book you were a different person than you are in this moment. If there is an old thought or two lingering on, let it go. The new you has a choice in who to be. Don't change yourself for others, or for their thoughts.

So you have fear, anger, sadness, regret, etc...accept it. It's there. There is no need to fight your thoughts, just thank them and let them go. Once you can get okay with how things are, you can work on changing them. Start telling yourself that you are proud of yourself. Tell yourself you love yourself just as you are. We like to worry about what other people will think of us when really we are just judging ourselves. When you can see your judgments, you can work on changing how you see yourself.

Comparison

Have you ever wished to be somebody else? Maybe you've dreamt of being a celebrity, or one of the 'cool' kids at school, or maybe a professional athlete. The real question is, are you happy with yourself?

You're right; you are never going to be like those other people. You are you. Our lives are our own to live. Nobody else can live your life. And only you can figure out how to be happy with the story you're living. Only you can get okay with what your talents are; what gifts you can share with the world.

Life is what you choose to think of it as. You can be whatever you want to be, do whatever you want to do, but then also accept the things you *can* do, in this moment. We like to think other people have it easier than us when we perceive our lives as being difficult. We think we have to do better than our parents. There is no such thing as better or worse, only what is best. Be yourself and do your best in the moment.

It can be hard not caring what other people think. We want to fit in. We want to be liked. We want to be loved. We don't want to rock the boat. But what do we is sacrifice our happiness every time we care about someone else's thoughts. We sacrifice a piece of ourselves.

You can't stop worrying about what other people think of you until you figure out why you care, and why you can't love yourself just as you are.

Sometimes I still care about what people think of me. Especially in new situations I have old thoughts re-surface. But I also remember how ridiculous it is to care about that, and that helps. I'm not saying it goes away easy, caring about the thoughts of others. But it does lessen over time. Every new moment is a chance to practice the new you, the new thoughts and the new beliefs that you want to define your life's story.

Body Issues

One of the hardest things about living in the now is being okay with the parts of your story that you can't change. Like the body you were born into. One way to get okay with your body is to think of it as simply the vessel that allows you to experience life. Each experience is unique. Our vessels are unique.

Change your thoughts regarding your body. You are not what you eat. You are not the number on the clothes you wear. Find something you *do* like about your body. There is always something to love about you. I had to start with my eyes. My eyes were easy to love for their color. Add on to your list when you become more comfortable in your vessel.

Ultimately we are not our bodies. We aren't even our minds. Learn to listen to the body as a separate being, a separate consciousness. It'll want certain foods because it may not be getting certain vitamins or minerals it needs to function. It'll want other foods for how they make it feel.

The body lives moment to moment just like the rest of us. Honor that, without judgment. Just know the difference when it's your ego that wants something. We often feed our emotions. Why do you want that piece of cake? Stop and think about what you are thinking. Are you bored, sad, or does that cake just look really good right now?

Establish a friendship and respect with your body. Feed your body love. Tell your body you love it. Let go of everything that isn't love for yourself, your body, your mind, and your soul. No matter what your vessel looks like, no matter how it functions, it provides the opportunity to experience everything. It heals itself when it gets injured, it makes sure we keep breathing as we rest, it does a lot of things we don't realize on a moment to moment basis. Take time to acknowledge your body for what it does for you.

Establish Trust

It is hard to put yourself out there. It is hard to be yourself at times. All the doubt, fear and past memories can resurface at any moment like a test. Be aware of these thoughts. Society tells us to be ourselves, and on the other hand it wants us to be like everybody else. Trust that the real you is exactly who you need to be in this moment. You are not wrong for being yourself.

Establish trust by believing in yourself, in who you truly are. Trust your own feelings. Trust what your heart wants and not what your ego mind is telling you. So what if other people don't like you? That is their problem, not yours. The only person who needs to like you is you.

You can perform your own lie-detector test to determine how you really see yourself. Close your eyes, put your hands on your heart, and say aloud things you know to be true and things you know not to be true. Your voice will tell you what you truly believe. Start with your name and other 'facts' about yourself, and then say something like *I am beautiful* or *I love myself*. Notice how and if your voice changes in everything you try to say aloud. Often what we can't easily say tells us more than what we can say.

SAYING NO WITH LOVE

It is okay to say: *no I am not going to do what I did in the past*. Will you continue to do what is easy or will you choose to say: *no, that's not me anymore*? Can you take the steps towards the life you want and let go of what's holding you back? It's only the mind's perception that our choices are hard, that it is difficult to stand up for who we are, what we want, and how we choose to live our lives.

In order to maintain our happiness, we may have to establish boundaries. If you want to be in my world then this is what you have to do: you have to come from a place of honor and respect. Require others to take responsibility for their reality as you do yours. One can't save the whole world, so your priority is your own well-being.

If other people in your life don't want to respect your choices or your decision to live in the now and let go of the past and the future, then that is their issue. You have to decide if you need to move forward in your journey without them.

Everyone has a personal space bubble. Imagine yourself in an invisible, energetic bubble around your body. When you feel angry, your personal space bubble exudes anger. When you feel happy, your bubble exudes happiness.

You may feel uncomfortable around people, or their energy, based on the energy within their bubble. And sometimes you may not want to be around them at all. Likewise, others may not want to be around you if you're working through some anger, or sadness, etc. Your energy attracts and repels others. You'll find that your relationships will change when you start to recognize the energy around you.

So what energy would you like to radiate to the world? When you love who you are, your energy will reflect that. You can choose how people see you by choosing how to see yourself. If you come from a place of love, respect, and honor for yourself and your reality, others will see you in that light because you respect and honor yourself.

Everyone is worthy of love. *You* are worthy of love. Love yourself and expect others to love themselves before loving you as well.

Confidence

It's ok to be afraid to be yourself. It's what you do with that fear that defines who you are as a person. What's the worst that can happen? So what if that person doesn't like me. So what if no one understands me. Could you live with that one person hating you? Could you live with the whole world hating you for being you? And I mean the real you.

It's a continuous process to overcome our fears. Don't beat yourself up. Confidence takes practice. Living in the now takes practice. I wish it was an instantaneous change, like flipping a light switch on. But it's not. If you really want to live in the moment, consciously, you have to put in the work. It is easy to go back to sleep, to go back on auto-pilot, to let the universe run its course while you wait for things to happen. Sometimes it takes a giant leap of faith to trust yourself to choose the details of your own story.

There will always be the little voice at the back of your mind that says you can't do something, that you shouldn't do that or say that, or that you shouldn't wear, eat, drink that. It's hard to keep standing up for yourself. Sometimes I give in to those thoughts. And that is okay too. I just keep working on it, building my confidence. No worries, no regrets. I believe that everything is as it should be and I try to be the best version of myself in every moment.

Think of everything as a game. When you think you can't do something, all you need to do is just practice. You can do anything you set your mind to, i.e. work with your thoughts about it. Practice whatever it is. Believe you can do it.

Respect

"There are hundreds of paths up the mountain, all leading to the same place; so it doesn't matter which path you take. The only person wasting time is the one who runs around the mountain telling everything that his or her path is wrong."
-Hindu Proverb

We all have choice. Some call it free will. Choose to be the master of your own thoughts, or choose to let your thoughts govern your life. Respect other people's choices as well. Some people like things chosen for them, and that is okay too. Your path is not better than anybody else's path. Your path is your own to walk, to live.

Respect yourself as you respect others. We all have our own beliefs, our own thoughts, and our own choices to make. Everyone can be who they want to be. Everyone can believe what they want to believe. As you focus on yourself and your journey, be mindful of your needs while being mindful of other's needs. Have compassion for all living things and remember that what's in your best interest may not be best for another.

Everyone has fear. Everyone has pain. We're all working through our own stories. Be kind. Communicate from a place of respect. If you are unsure how to treat another being, put yourself in their shoes. How would you want to be treated? Do you want your choices to be respected? Do you want to live your life in peace?

ALLOWING YOURSELF TO BE HAPPY

Living in the now is being aware of and recognizing what you allow in your life. Allow yourself to believe in something new. Allow yourself to let go of the past, to let go of that which no longer serves your best interest from this moment on. Give yourself permission to not care what people think. Give yourself permission to be happy in every moment. You hold all the power and remembering that power is happiness.

Instead of saying "I can't eat that," change it to "I'm not allowed to eat that" and see how it feels. Who isn't allowing you to eat that? Why not? Maybe you're not allowing yourself to eat dessert because you think you'll get fat. I've been there. If thoughts are so powerful, do you think chocolate cake could make you lose weight if you truly believed it would? Food is just energy after all, and we choose what energy we want to fuel our bodies. The trick is not to give yourself a hard time for enjoying it. You'll find your diet will start to change when you practice conscious eating in the moment. What you allow and don't allow in your body will change too.

One tip to losing weight is to not take food away (the ego has issues with this), but instead introduce new foods and slowly remove what no longer feels good.

Allow yourself to experience new things. Allow yourself to be happy when you are living life the way you want to. It is your choice to let others affect what you think.

And why is it so important to make someone else happy? By all means make someone else happy, or try to. Just don't be disappointed when that person doesn't stay happy. That is not your fault, problem, or concern. Only we can make ourselves happy and stay happy. It's all in the mind, the individual mind.

Happiness isn't something to pursue. It doesn't exist out there somewhere. It exists within us always. You cannot find something that you already have. So be happy for no reason. The ego likes reasons, so make up one if you need to. Remember that you are just as important. Never forget that your happiness comes first, that you deserve to be happy. We all do.

Being happy doesn't mean that everything is perfect. Being happy means that you are okay with whatever happens. If you're not happy, it could mean that you have been unable to speak your truth. Speaking your truth and proving it are two different things. There is no need to prove anything to anyone. Your truth is your own. As long as you know it, that is all that matters.

Honor

What story do you tell yourself? What story do you tell others? How often do you change your story for others? Honor is staying true to one's self. Changing your needs based on your perception of others is compromising yourself. Your needs, your desires, are just as important. Honor your story, your journey, in every moment. Honor the needs of others as well.

Listen to the words you tell yourself. Look at how you live your life. Action and words need to match in order to be truthful. You can't say one thing about yourself and do another. You can't say you're beautiful and then deny yourself a meal because you think you're too fat. Remember to be honorable to yourself by speaking and living your truth.

Most of all, quit lying to yourself. Are you being true to your word? Are you happy? It is okay to answer no. The real question is; do you *want* to be true to yourself? Do you want to be happy? We often lie to ourselves more than we lie to other people. We say we don't really want to do that thing, but really it's just fear. Can you look at your thoughts and *truly* not believe them anymore? Can you embrace the change you need?

Practice honoring your journey by being raw, real and honest in every moment. Remember that our needs can change in any moment. Honor that change. Remember that you can choose something different in any moment. There is no need to judge yourself, your thoughts, or your journey anymore. Honor yourself each and every day by doing what you need to do, when you need to do it.

The Caretaker Role

Caretakers make sure everyone else is okay. Caretakers like to play the role of everyone's mother. Caretakers are more concerned with others than of themselves. Caretakers put others' happiness before their own. There is a difference between caretaking and compassion. You can have compassion for others' choices to do things their way, to have responsibility for themselves, even if you perceive them as wrong. Suffering is a choice after all. The only person you truly can take care of is yourself.

Do you feel obligated to take care of someone else? Obligation isn't necessarily honor. Honor comes from the heart, with love and compassion. Ignoring others' needs to experience life as they see fit isn't compassion. You can have compassion for someone even if they choose to suffer.

The only thing you can do for another is ask questions. Ask them why they feel that way, why they do the things that they do, why they think what they think. Make them question their reality as you do yours. They may not know they can change their thoughts, and you can remind them of that, but they have to do the work themselves, as you do yours. No one can do the work for you.

Remember your own happiness and your own needs. It is easy to forget about yourself in the service of others. When one keeps ignoring their own needs, they can create feelings of anger, resentment, sadness, regret, etc.

I experienced the beginnings of resentment when I was taking care of a sick family member. I ended up being on the clock 24/7 taking care of this person. I'm the kind of person who loves her sleep, so getting less than twenty hours of sleep over the course of a week was a new experience for me. There is a difference between selfishness and taking care of your needs first. This person questioned my need to sleep. I wasn't even allowed to sleep while they slept because they were afraid they would wake up at any moment and need help.

In short, stand up for your needs. Your happiness is important. Your needs matter. *You* matter. Even if you have to tell yourself, that just after this moment or as soon as you can, we will get you taken care of, acknowledge your needs. Be aware of your needs while you are taking care of others. It can be hard at times. It is hard to tell someone they need to figure something out because you need to do something like sleep. Remember to take time for yourself. You can focus on your journey without being selfish. Respect your journey. Honor your journey. Love your journey to living in the now.

FINAL THOUGHTS

EVERYTHING IS A GIFT

What if I told you that everything in your life is a gift, would you believe it? What do you have to be grateful for in your life? Can you look beyond the experiences you perceive as 'bad' and believe that everything happens for a reason? It's okay if you don't.

Getting to the mindset that every experience is a gift, an opportunity to grow and expand our possibilities in life, can be hard to do. If you can see anger as a gift, a gift that shows you where your thoughts need adjustment, then you can let go of that anger quicker by not letting it affect you the same way in that moment.

Your breath is a gift. Your heartbeat is a gift. We can rest the body and mind, drift off to sleep, and wake up having breathed the entire time. Start with the things you can easily see as gifts in your life. Get into the mindset of accepting gifts from reality. Ask for them even. You'd be surprised what you can call forth in your life. It is your story after all.

Tell the stars good night, tell the sun good morning. Every word counts. Make every day a love-filled day. You get what you give. And don't just think positive, expect positive. If there is just one expectation we should have, it would be that everything is perfect just as it is. Every experience is perfect just as it happens.

A Final Story

Have you heard of the story of the two patients in a hospital room? The man by the window was well enough to prop himself up every day to peer out the window and describe to the other man, who was immobilized in the bed next to him, unable to see out the window, everything he could see outside.

Every day the man by the window would describe what he saw; one day it was a lush park with a pond and ducks and the next day he described was a parade passing in the distance. He described everything he saw in vivid detail. The man in the next bed looked forward to hearing about the world outside as he got better.

One day the nurse discovered the man by the window had passed quietly in the night and soon the other man was well enough to be moved to the window as he could prop himself and look around now. With his first glimpse out the window he was utterly confused.

All he could see was the wall across the courtyard into another hospital room. The nurse explained that the man by the window was blind. When the man asked why someone would make up such stories about the outside world, all she could reply was that perhaps he wanted to encourage him as best he could.

The man in the other bed could have gotten angry with the man by the window for lying to him. Or he could be grateful that someone cared enough to make him feel better, no matter the cost. The blind man by the window spent his time, his energy, making up wonderful stories in his head on behalf of the well-being of the man in the next bed.

Words have power. The stories we tell have power. Try to see the good in everything. Try to see the gifts the universe sends you in every moment, even if you're staring out the window and all you see is a brick wall.

GETTING STUCK IN A MOMENT

There is no such thing as getting stuck. We just feel stuck. Honor how you feel in every moment. There will be times you don't feel like doing anything. And there will be times when you feel like you've accomplished so many things: you've released old programs, old thoughts, challenged and overcame your fears. Just go with the flow of how you feel in each and every moment.

Living in the now is a new way of being. Give yourself a break. Don't give yourself a hard time anymore, we've all done that plenty throughout our lives. Just move on. Get okay with whatever happened and move on to the next moment. We don't fully understand things until after they happen. Getting 'stuck' may just be another experience you need to have, and when you realize you are having that experience you can choose to think differently in that moment.

We can get stuck in an idea, a certain belief system. We can refuse to listen to other options. This shuts down our growth. We're meant to consider all the possibilities in life.

There is no such thing as making a living the 'right' way. There is not just one way to accomplish a task. Expand your horizons. Expand your possibilities. If you can think of more options, more choices will become available to you. Everything is possible.

Remember, there nothing is wrong with you. There is nothing

to "fix". Getting yourself 'back on the right track' implies you've been on the wrong one. There is no need such thing as the wrong path. Just choose a different track, a different path, to walk if you want. No one said you had to stay on the same path your whole life. Explore your story, travel many roads.

If you feel you can't change your reality to something you truly want just yet, then start by changing the thoughts about your current situation. Question why you can't get that new job, move to another place, end a relationship or start one, or whatever it is you want to change. Finding the answers may tell you what thoughts and beliefs are running around in the background. It gives you a starting point. You can change your reality by first believing you can.

As humans, we have an expectation to be doing something, anything. Be okay with doing nothing. Say you're not going to have any expectations. In this moment you are doing exactly what you need to be doing. Sitting on the couch playing video games may be what you need to be doing. When you are done with that thing, move on to the next one. No judgments. No attachments.

Pay attention to the words you use in moments when you feel stuck.

Instead of saying 'I always do that...' rephrase it to say 'I always *did* that...' Start thinking in terms of the old you and the new you. The old you will try to gain control of your life again, but you can choose to let it go and change, or to hold on to your past. Sometimes we get ourselves stuck on purpose. The ego, and its self-defense mechanism, will try to get you to think of something, anything, else that will distract you from letting go and discovering your true self.

Are you running away from your problems? Your thoughts? Just be aware of why you're thinking something. Awareness is the first step to consciousness.

Questions to ask yourself when you feel stuck:

What do you want to let go of?
What do you fear?
What's holding you back?
What, or who, are you attached to?
Where are you changing and compromising yourself?
Do you have regrets?
Why do you regret that?
Why are you angry?
What are you grateful for in this moment?
What are you waiting for?
What is the worst that can happen?
Can you get okay with it?
What are you thinking right now?
Are you happy?
Do you, truly, love yourself?
Can you?

Sometimes you won't know the answer right away. And that is okay. All you have to do is ask.

FINAL THOUGHTS

Yesterday and tomorrow are just words, words with thoughts attached. You can let the past thoughts haunt you in every moment, or you can choose to let them go. Words may have power, but it is us who give them that power. Take the power away from a word, a thought, and it can no longer affect you in the same way again. Give thoughts new meaning by changing the words attached to them. Thoughts can be freeing or they can be your prison, it is your choice.

If there is just one thing I hoped you would get out of this book, it would be to question your thoughts. Why do you think the way you do? The answer should surprise you. And that is a good thing. Just notice what you are saying to yourself, and what you say to others. Be careful what you say to yourself, because you *are* listening. Joking about thoughts you have isn't enough to change. One can't joke about being sick or ugly because that just reinforces the automatic program.

Break down those thoughts, see where they come from, and logically not believe them anymore. Remember that the ego is logical. You also have to convince your ego that you are worthy of love, beauty and happiness.

Choose what you want to believe now. Those who believe in limits are limited. Forget that you are a flawed human. Think something new about yourself. Believe in the new. If you think you'll never get well, then you won't. If you think you'll never lose weight, then you won't. If you think you are fat, then you are fat. Who is telling you that you're fat? There is no such thing as too fat or too skinny. It is all a perception of the mind, and every mind is different.

There is no instantaneous change to living in the now. It needs a little work, work on your end. Choose in every moment what life you wish to live. It is our choices that truly define who we are. Let go of the past. Stop worrying about the future. Trust in your perfection, a perfection you embody in every moment. Trust that happiness exists within you always. You just have to remember.

Your feelings are going to drive your reality now. What am I supposed to do today? What do I feel like doing today? Be okay with whatever you are experiencing right now.

Everything happens for a reason. You read this book for a reason. You may not know why you do everything you do, or why things happen in your life. Don't judge what you experience.

Be ready. Be open to the new, the change, and the now. Now it is time to be a conscious creator of your own reality. Make it a priority to have fun. Take the pressure off yourself. You *are* accomplishing things in every moment.

Just play with new ideas. You don't have to believe them right away, or at all in fact. Just leave yourself open to new possibilities, to new truths. What is true for you is all that matters. Truth is subjective after all. Find your truth and live it.

Thank you and I love you

ABOUT THE AUTHOR

Elizabeth Crooks is a writer, author, artist and guide who shares her knowledge of consciousness and the human experience, emphasizing the art of mindfulness and living from the heart.

She holds a Bachelor of Metaphysical Sciences degree (B.Msc.) from the University of Metaphysics Sciences, and is a certified Reiki Master with years of energy work experience.

When she is not sharing her knowledge through writings she spends her time reading, traveling, walking in nature, creating art, and doodling in love. She is a published author on books pertaining to metaphysical sciences and personal growth as well as coloring books for both adults and children.

For more information, please visit:
www.elizabeth-crooks.com

www.ingramcontent.com/pod-product-compliance
Lightning Source LLC
Chambersburg PA
CBHW060938040426
42445CB00011B/918